D0334873

GARDENING

Tips & Hints

ABOUT THE AUTHOR

Margaret Briggs was a teacher for 30 years, working in Kent, North Yorkshire, Sussex and Germany. She has always enjoyed gardening and has grown plants both to eat and look at for all her adult life.

Since leaving teaching she has had more time for gardening and has embarked on a second career as a freelance writer, researcher and editor, alongside her writer husband, Lol. Six years ago the couple bought a dilapidated house in SW France, allowing even more scope for gardening and their love of the French language and culture. The house is now restored and Margaret and Lol divide their time between Sussex and the Gironde, with two contrasting gardens to develop.

Margaret's first book, *Vinegar 1001 Practical Uses*, was published in 2005.

GARDENING
Tips & Hints

Margaret Briggs

Abbeydale Press

ISBN 1-86147-195-5
978-1-86147-195-6

Published by Abbeydale Press
an imprint of Bookmart Ltd
Registered number 2372865
Trading as Bookmart Ltd
Blaby Road, Wigston, Leicester

CONTENTS

PART 2 THE ART OF GOOD GARDENING

Introduction

Congratulations on becoming the custodian of your own garden space — or commiserations if you have reluctantly taken over a house or flat with a garden and you're not yet a gardening fan. Gardening is an activity that has often been seen as something for the middle aged and elderly; something the young people in my family have always loathed by association with a grown-up activity, but there's a thaw in the air. It seems to be connected with having your own living space and a small piece of land that you are totally responsible for.

I had my first taste of gardening at the age of about seven, when we visited my grandparents. My granddad grew a variety of vegetables and flowers in the back garden, and I always had the job of helping plant the runner beans and potatoes. It was magic, getting dirty, digging holes with a dibber and watering everything in sight. My parents became increasingly keen gardeners as they got older, although I don't remember my brother showing any interest at all. Nowadays, he's the one with two allotments and bigger and better vegetables than ours. My husband loathed the whole concept of spending time digging and, especially, weeding. Even he has mellowed a lot over the years, having seen how we can easily transform areas of land, sometimes creating from scratch. This is just as well, as he does most of the heavy work!

The benefits are immediate and numerous. Who doesn't feel good about cutting some edges on a scraggy bit of lawn, or seeing flowers where there was only dead vegetation and litter? Even the least keen gardener has to admit to a sneaky feeling of self-satisfaction at this small transformation, and woe betide the neighbouring moggy who dares to investigate the newly turned soil, even if you are a cat lover by nature!

This book will take you through all you need to know about beginning to make a garden. With any luck, you're

already keen and this hasn't been foisted on you.
If you belong to the latter group, I hope to offer you
encouragement, time- and effort-saving suggestions.
It doesn't have to absorb a huge amount of your leisure
time or finances, but that's up to you. It can give you
valuable thinking time, gentle exercise, a place to sit and
veg out and a sense of enormous satisfaction and well-
being. If you're really concerned about your diet and
lifestyle, gardening can give you added benefits:
delicious, home-grown vegetables and fruit for little
outlay, a feast of colour, fragrance and tactile
experiences, plus a full physical workout into the bargain.

So before you decide to pave the front garden, or deck
the entire backyard, please read on. You might save
a lot of money, effort and time, and begin to see the
environmental benefits available thanks to a modest
input.

PART 1
MAKING A PRACTICAL START

Chapter 1

Plant Factories
The Science of Plant Growth

Everyone has to start somewhere, so instead of thinking about what to do first or how to plan your garden, start with a tidy up. You may be surprised by what you find. Old shopping trolleys and bikes spring to mind here — as our introduction to our current garden — but that's not always the case. Someone once told me to do nothing but tidy for the first year, until you see what's planted already, but I've always been too impatient for that.
I do think the idea of living in a house for three months before deciding on major decoration or renovation projects is a good idea to transfer to the garden, though. If you move during the winter, this period might need to be longer, so that, with the coming of spring and summer, you give dormant plants and bulbs the chance to show what they can do for you. If you've acquired a brand new plot on a building site, you have my sympathies, but don't despair. At least you have a blank canvas to work on, although you'll need to spend a bit more time digging up building rubble and clay first. Don't be too enthusiastic, though I recall my brother as a teenager, digging furiously to impress someone or other, while helping my parents dig a pond in their newish garden. Beneath the buried rubble he hit the main sewer and caused a major stink!

Clearing up rubbish, cutting the grass and clipping edges and hedges can make a world of difference. Get out the worst of the weeds. The area will look better straight away. Then you can see what's worth keeping and decide on any new features and plants of your own. It's easier and much more fun to let the garden 'grow up' around you gradually. Rushing into major changes can result in wasted time, effort and money.

HOW PLANTS GROW

Plants are like factories; from the outside they look relatively inactive, but there's a lot going on inside. During daylight hours the green pigment in plants called chlorophyll traps sunlight and uses it as a source of energy to turn carbon dioxide from the air and water from the soil into carbohydrates. These are stored as starch in the roots and leaves. This process is called photosynthesis. At the same time, oxygen is produced as a waste product and is diffused into the air from the leaves. Plants respire rather like animals, taking in oxygen and giving off carbon dioxide. During the day more carbon dioxide is taken in during photosynthesis than is given out during respiration. During the night, when photosynthesis ceases, respiration is the only process going on.

Using the basic raw ingredients of minerals, air and water, plants manufacture hormones that control the ways different parts of the plant turn tissue into roots, buds and leaves. Forty or so different minerals are taken up in the water absorbed through the roots. Plants also make their own colouring materials, fragrances and a wide range of other sophisticated chemicals, including those which repel certain predators.

Plants make their own structure, laying down lignin (wood) to support tall constructions such as trees and woody shrubs, stems of perennial plants, cabbage stalks, etc. Cellulose makes cell walls to build new leaves and other structures.

Water constantly evaporates from tiny pores in the leaves. This is called transpiration. If a plant loses more water than it takes up from the soil, it starts to wilt.

The ultimate aim of any plant is to reproduce itself by shedding ripe seeds. To produce a wide range of offspring, many plants bear attractive flowers with pollen or nectar to attract insects that cross-pollinate them, creating new genetic combinations. When ripe, these seeds are scattered by some ingenious methods.

Seed dispersal takes different forms, for example wind, explosion or enlisting the help of animals and birds. Trees like sycamore and acer varieties have winged seedpods to spin away on the breeze. Others like a good explosion, like the pea family. Tasty fruit ensures that animals or birds swallow the seeds of various plants and deposit them further way, along with their own supply of manure. Tomato seeds are about the most indestructible and can be found in sewage plants quite frequently. Other seeds, like burdock, have small hooks forming burs which attach themselves to passing legs or sides for transportation. Self-sown seedlings can be a real help with the budget when starting out, or when you want to increase your stock of plants. Just don't be surprised if the seedlings don't look exactly like the older, parent plants.

Chapter 2

Doing the Groundwork
Soil

Soil doesn't look very exciting, but it provides the heart of the garden. It is like a supermarket, supplying water, air and food to the plants it has growing in it. It also gives roots something to grip onto, so that they can hold plants upright. To garden successfully, you need to know a bit about your soil. This can vary from garden to garden, or, in some cases, within the garden itself. So although looking over the fence at the neighbours' plots can be helpful when you want some idea of what grows and what doesn't, you can't just assume that your plot has been looked after to the same extent.

SOIL IS NOT DEAD

There is plenty going on underground which is essential for the smooth running of the garden. Soil contains billions of microscopic organisms, some of which are beneficial and some harmful. The beneficial bacteria eat plant and animal remains, turning them into plant food. Digging plenty of garden compost and manure into the soil is a good way of adding extra good bacteria, but don't put diseased plants onto the compost heap, otherwise the harmful organisms will be spread when you use the compost. There is more information on composting on page 28.

ENCOURAGE THE WORMS

Worms are extremely good for the soil as their burrows make tiny airways that aerate the soil and also help to drain water away. They are the labour force you want to encourage. They eat their way through the job, allowing enormous quantities of soil and organic matter to pass through their bodies. This is the first stage in breaking down organic matter into humus. The worm casts you see on the surface are just the tip of the iceberg; they are deposited within the soil as well and play an important part in forming soil crumbs. They are rich in minerals, micro-organisms and nutrients which the plants can use straight away. Finally, the worms become a fertiliser themselves. Their bodies are a rich source of protein (ask any bird) and when they die and are recycled they return nitrogen to the soil. Basically then, they are the most natural fertiliser you can get, so do your best to encourage them! We disturb hundreds of them every time we add more kitchen peelings to the compost bins in our garden. Lovely grub!

DIGGING FOR SUCCESS

Gardening isn't a natural activity. In the wild you won't find the same variety of plants growing in a particular area as you will in a garden. We want our gardens to grow a huge variety of flowers, fruit or vegetables in close proximity and expect them to look good all the time. We take a lot out of the soil by harvesting crops, which would otherwise be returned to the soil for future enrichment. Even pruning, grass cutting, weeding, collecting dead leaves and plants from the soil impoverish the soil further. The general rule should be to always put something back after you've borrowed from the soil bank.

Digging helps to aerate the soil and expose pests to predators. It can also encourage the wildlife that eats vast quantities of pests. We have a resident robin, who sits so close by when we're digging that I always worry that he'll get hit by the spade or fork. Digging also gives you a chance to add humus-forming manure or compost to your soil. For heavy clay soils this is a must as it will improve the structure. Autumn and winter are the best times for digging, although if you're like us, you'll still be at it in the spring.

THE NO DIG APPROACH

There is a school of thought that says that you can improve the soil without a lot of heaving soil around by digging it. We tried this once, but I can't say it was a great success on the vegetable front, although having heavy clay soil to start with isn't ideal. It's worth a try in a small area, though, or if you suffer from back problems. Spread manure or compost on the surface in a layer up to 15 cm (6 in) deep. As far as possible, keep the area continually mulched. Scrape away the mulch to plant seedlings or to sow seeds. You need a lot of mulch for this, so try it after you've got the compost bin going. See page 28 for more details. Avoid walking on the mulch as this will compact the soil, prevent water draining away and make it harder for roots to penetrate and develop.

DIGGING A SMALL AREA

Use a spade for normal digging, but choose a fork to loosen ground that has already been turned over, or when perennial weeds are a persistent problem. A fork is less likely to slice through the roots and leave pieces behind to grow again. By shaking the soil through the prongs it's easier to remove troublesome weeds. See advice on tools on page 34.

For a small area of ground, use a spade and drive into the ground at right angles. Push as far in as possible without having to push it in with your foot, 15—20 cm (6—8 in) is far enough. Don't be tempted to be too ambitious with quantity of soil, or you might end up with back problems. If you're not used to physical labour, then be extra careful and work up gradually. As you get better at it, then you can use your foot more. Pull back on the handle, using it as a lever to loosen the bite of soil. Lift the spadeful of soil, keeping your back as straight as possible and doing the lifting with your knees. Flick the soil off, inverting it to bury the weeds. If you're lucky, most annual weeds will be killed, and will decompose. Perennials like dock, dandelion and nettles, however, must be removed to prevent spread. Throw the soil forward slightly as you work, then rake it level when preparing the soil for planting. When you reach the end of a row, work back in the opposite direction.

WHAT SORT OF SOIL?

We've 'looked after' many gardens in different parts of the country over the last 30 years. That's the fun of moving house and area. We've had all soil types but mostly, it seems, the hard work variety. All gardens can be hard work, and digging can't really be avoided. The advantage of chalk soils is that drainage isn't a problem, but then again, retaining moisture can be a disadvantage in dry weather. Our current garden in Sussex is on the edge of a marshland. Lovely views, old mature garden, we thought we'd got it made until we tried digging into solid clay. After 13 years we're finally winning, but we've only achieved this by a lot of hard work and digging in lots of compost, leaf mould, bonfire ash and sand. Even then, there are flower borders we only get to every so often, and there are distinct layers of clay and loamy soil, on the sloping site. What a contrast then, to inherit a garden in south-west France which had been untouched for about 12 years. What joy to cultivate a sandy loam! The disadvantages are that the area is prone to drought and the soil is incredibly well drained, but after years of heavy digging, this is a doddle. It just means you have to be aware of soil type all the time and plant accordingly.

Soil may be acid, neutral or alkaline. Some plants prefer one type, although most popular plants are fairly easy going and grow in any kind except extremes. You can buy a test kit in a garden centre which will check the pH, or the scale used to show acidity or alkalinity, and this might be a good idea if you move to a new garden, but why not just grow what the soil likes, and settle for the odd fussy plant in a container?

So, whatever pH or soil type, there's no real substitute for digging to:

- AERATE THE SOIL

- HELP DRAINAGE

- HELP THE WORMS

- WORK IN ORGANIC MATTER

If you're not the scientific type, try this handy test:

Appearance	Diagnosis	Remedy
Dries out fast after rain. Puddles vanish quickly. Gritty feel. Light in colour.	Sandy soil	Use plenty of organic matter.
Sticky when wet. Boggy in winter. Puddles last ages. Dries out eventually into hard lumps. Large cracks appear when dry.	Clay soil	Use plenty of organic matter, plus sand, grit, ash or bark chippings.
Dries out quickly after rain. Pale colour, stony. Very thin layer of soil over white, crumbly rock.	Chalky soil	Use plenty of organic matter.
Dark brown breadcrumbs. Old garden, well established. Old grassland, recently dug over.	Loamy soil	Maintain fertility by good cultivation.

Chapter 3

Doing the
Groundwork
Water and Watering

Although they look fairly solid, green plants are about 95 per cent water. They wilt when not watered. Water also provides plants with their own internal transport system, moving nutrients and manufactured carbohydrates and hormones to wherever they are needed, in order for the plant to grow, survive and reproduce.

LEAVE IT TO NATURE

In the wild, plants get by without being watered. Our garden in France hadn't been cultivated or watered for 12 years, but there were climbing roses, vines, lilacs and bulbs surviving, despite the monster brambles. Even in very dry conditions, these plants, with their well-established root systems, survived a hurricane, several years of drought and the odd patches of sub-zero temperatures. That's why the Bordeaux area is renowned for its vineyards: the vines have roots which go down 10 metres in the sandy soil, in search of water. As their roots remain undamaged by digging, they can produce grapes, with a bit of help, for 50 years or more. The vines in our garden, however, were not good-looking specimens: raggy and surviving to produce very small grapes, not good enough for a garden.

DEMANDING GARDENERS

In gardens we don't want to grow the plants that appear naturally, i.e. those commonly called weeds. We want man-made cultivars and exotic species which have been artificially propagated, pricked out, potted and transplanted. Because the roots have been damaged by interference, cultivated plants develop smaller, shallower root systems. Because they are growing away from their natural environment, they are never as robust as native species, but we still want them to grow strong and look more attractive. Watering is one way of helping them to do better.

CONSERVATION

However small your garden, there'll be times when you need a supply of water to keep plants growing and producing flowers or vegetables. Most established plants can survive in the ground with little in the way of artificial watering, either from a watering can or hosepipe. Even if you live in an area where water is plentiful and you don't suffer regular hosepipe bans as soon as the sun warms up, you don't really want the expense of additional water bills, if you're a new homeowner. Saving water is becoming more urgent with the onset of drier summers, so one practical way of cutting the bills and watering as and when the need arises is to use rainwater.

NO BUTTS?

Installing water butts, with lids and taps, is a simple way of collecting water from the roof. If you cut a section of drainpipe with a hacksaw and insert a rainwater diverter, the diverter sends the water to the butt until the butt is full, then lets it continue down the pipe to the normal outlet. We have a pair of butts connected to each other from a roof downspout situated alongside a greenhouse. These two 100-litre containers have lids which are childproof and keep out most insects as well. The initial outlay has been recouped every year in a saving of water bills, which, in an area with water meters installed many years ago, has to be good news. Other butts are sited around the garden to avoid carrying watering cans long distances. Even a small roof area, for instance a greenhouse or shed roof, can provide quite a useful amount of water for little effort. Simply attach some guttering to the side of the roof and extend the end of the guttering over a container. We use old dustbins, and kitchen waste bins for smaller quantities. A lid is desirable to prevent algae forming and to keep it smelling okay. The downsides are that you are provided with a great breeding ground for midges and that rainwater tends to be slightly acidic, so is not good for acid-hating plants.

The upside, though, outweighs the disadvantages, in that you won't be tempted to sneak out in the dark to use that lovely new hose on a reel that cost the earth.

SENSIBLE PLANTING

Much more sensible than giving yourself the extra fuss of watering those lush, thirsty exotics is to 'go with the flow': to select plants that will thrive in particular conditions without excessive watering. You can tell a lot about plants by looking at their leaves. In hot dry areas where water is short, plants have evolved ways of retaining moisture with waxy skins, furry leaves or silver coloration that reflects light. Desert plants have often given up on leaves altogether in place of tough spines instead. In damp, humid places plants like hostas don't have to worry about saving water, so they have large, thin leaves. Tropical plants, which make up the majority of houseplants, have glossy leaves with drip tips to drain off excess water.

DRIP FEEDS

If, however, you are new to gardening, but don't have any problem with finances, you could go for a small-scale sprinkler system or drip watering system. This avoids having to carry cans around and can be better for the plants. With a drip feed system you can run both spray and nozzles off the same system. Connect the master unit to a hose from the mains. The master unit reduces the water pressure and contains a removable filter. Run the main supply where it won't be too visible, e.g. under a hedge or buried in the soil. Connect smaller branch tubes wherever you need to take water to a particular part of the garden. Drip feed heads can be used to water containers and individual plants in a border. If you have gone this far, you might as well go for broke and get a tap computer as well, which will save you the trouble and turn the water supply on and off at programmed times, even when you are away on holiday.

SPRINKLERS

A spray head can be used for more general watering, such as flower beds or rows of vegetables, but beware! Once started, the plants will expect regular treatment, which may not be possible during periods of drought. All the oscillating static, rotating or pulse jet and static sprinklers in the world will be no good then. They sound and look fabulous and can be a lot of fun in hot weather, but we're talking gardening here!

SEEP HOSES

Seep hoses are designed to be laid along the ground for long-term watering. The tiny perforations deliver water slowly so that it seeps well into the soil. They are especially useful for irrigating rows of fruit or vegetables. Some are made of porous rubber and aren't very pretty

unless you bury them in a shallow trench 10—15 cm
(4—6 in) deep.

WAYS OF MAKING THE WATER GO FURTHER

MULCHING
This is a very good way of keeping moisture around the
roots of plants. Even drought-tolerant plants will need
some help until their roots are established, so water
plentifully when planting, then use black plastic, old
carpet or newspaper, covered with bark chips, grass
cuttings or shingle. More on this later.

GROUND COVER
Plant ground cover species thickly to prevent water loss
and to keep down the weeds, which will take all the
moisture from your beloved seedlings. Keep the weeds at
bay by hoeing or hand weeding.

GIVE THIRSTY PLANTS THEIR OWN SUPPLY
Cut off the end of a plastic water bottle and stick it neck
downwards into the ground, just above the roots. Fill the
bottle with water and let it seep down into the soil.

LINE CONTAINERS WITH PLASTIC
I always line hanging baskets with garden compost bags
turned black side out. The plastic is tougher. You can still
make it look better from the outside by pushing in a layer
of coir or, in our case, moss taken out of the lawn.

WATER-RETENTIVE GRANULES
These can be added when planting to preserve precious
moisture.

WATERING TIMES
In summer, water in the evenings so that plants have all
night to 'drink' before the sun comes out and dries up
moisture. Don't ever water plants while they are still in
strong sunlight as they will shrivel up.

In winter, water in the morning, if at all, so that plants
dry out before getting cold. This will make them less
prone to mildew.

TO WATER, OR NOT TO WATER

	Which plants?	**How?**
Water regularly	Plants in containers.	Fill to the brim and repeat until water trickles out through drainage holes.
As soon as soil starts to look dry	Shallow-rooted plants, e.g. bedding plants, herbs, vegetables and salad crops.	Soak thoroughly every 1–3 days.
When top 2.5–5 cm (1–2 in) soil dries out	Newly planted perennials, roses, trees, shrubs, climbers and new hedges.	Soak once or twice a week with hose or watering cans.
After several weeks of drought	Shallow-rooted shrubs, e.g. rhododendrons, camellias, climbers growing on walls, where the soil dries out faster.	Soak plants thoroughly with hose or cans. Don't bother with little often.
Don't bother	Established lawns, trees, shrubs, climbers and hedges.	Don't! They are better left for roots to 'dig deep'.

Chapter 4

Doing the Groundwork
Plant Foods, Composting and Feeding

Plants get much of what they need from the soil and from the compost and manure used to improve it, but in a crowded garden there might not be enough going back in. The bigger the garden, the more organic matter you'll be able to produce, but this isn't always possible in a small garden and anyway, you need to be able to produce before you can compost. High performance plants, such as long-flowering varieties or heavy-cropping kinds, need extra feeding, as do container-grown plants. I hold my hands up here as a bit of an organic fan.

PLANTS IN CONTAINERS

I don't do a lot of feeding of container plants, but I do give them good compost to grow in, plenty of rainwater when they need it and take care of them when they're looking tired or peaky by moving them into another position. Most, if not all, of our plants have been grown from seed or from cuttings. I use the same potting compost to start off all of these new plants, which contains plenty of nutrients for seedlings and cuttings, then repot into larger containers until planting in the ground. The remaining container-grown plants are likely to be heavy-cropping tomatoes or peppers, to be grown in the greenhouse. If you feel that your container plants need a supplement, use liquid or soluble feed once a week in place of plain water. Stop feeding when the plants stop growing.

PLANTS IN THE GROUND

Those plants which remain in the ground permanently — the shrubs and perennials — don't get the opportunity to get organic matter dug in, unless you decide to dig up the whole bed and replant (a drastic measure when you don't know your plants very well), so you can help them by sprinkling a general-purpose plant food or blood, fish and bone fertiliser over the bare soil between shrubs, roses, etc. This is best done in late spring, just before your plants start growing. Follow the rate recommended on the packet, and if you drop any fertiliser on the leaves of perennials, wash it off before it can scorch the leaves. Don't exceed the recommended quantities and spread evenly. If the weather is dry, hoe in the feed lightly and water in well. The job is made much easier if rain is due or the ground has been moistened by previous showers.

WHAT'S ON THE MENU?

Plants need different nutrients for different jobs. They need:

- NITROGEN for leaves
- POTASH for flowers and fruit
- PHOSPHATES for roots
- Minor trace elements such as IRON and MAGNESIUM

They need these minerals in the right proportions, but you're not expected to be a chemist here, so most fertilisers contain a balance of all three main nutrients. As a beginner you probably don't want to leave too much to chance, but I would urge you to wait and see what happens to your plants first. If the garden was well established there's probably more than enough in the ground already to sustain your plants until you see what's what. Trees and shrubs are best left and only fed in response to a known deficiency. If artificial fertilisers are overused chemical reactions can take place when the soil locks in the essential foods, which can make plants suffer deficiencies and cause diseases. Chemical fertilisers don't help the soil or supply food for worms, and we want to encourage the worms. Finally, they are expensive and use valuable resources to manufacture them. They can become pollutants, as shown by the high levels of nitrogen in rivers and water supplies in some parts of the country.

TYPES OF PLANT FOOD: SYNTHETIC OR INORGANIC FERTILISERS

LIQUID AND SOLUBLE FEEDS are taken up instantly by the plants and are the safest artificial feeds to use in pots and containers, as the nutrients are already in liquid form when you apply them. They are gulped down like a dose of salts, which is what they are. They may result in the plants putting on a spurt of soft sappy growth, which is prone to pest attacks and diseases. Use sparingly, measuring carefully and using at the recommended rate, or less.

GENERAL PURPOSE GRANULAR AND POWDER fertilisers are the cheapest. Use in spring or when preparing the ground before planting. Don't use in containers as they may scorch the roots. Balanced fertilisers, such as the formulation Growmore, contain all three main nutrients: nitrogen, phosphorus and potassium. Compound fertilisers are usually the same as balanced fertilisers, but don't always contain all three major nutrients.

SPECIALIST FEEDS are available for roses, ericaceous plants like rhododendrons (lime-hating), lawns, etc. They are manufactured to provide the right blend for those plants.

SLOW-RELEASE FEEDS are handy if you are forgetful. They come as feed sticks for containers, or as a single dose mixed into potting compost at the time of planting, which should last the whole season. Feed sticks work the same way, but may not last the season.

FOLIAR FEEDS are sprayed directly onto the plant leaves and are quickly taken in. They are used as very weak solutions to avoid scorching. Don't spray in hot sunny weather.

TYPES OF PLANT FOOD: ORGANIC FERTILISERS

These contain ingredients from natural origins. You can buy organic versions of a good range of granular and liquid feeds. Use gloves when handling all fertilisers.

BLOOD, FISH AND BONEMEAL sounds horrific and certainly made my daughter squeamish at a garden centre recently, but it contains all the major nutrients and doesn't look anything like its gory ingredients. The nitrogen content is released quickly.

BONEMEAL is a popular slow-acting fertiliser containing mainly phosphorus, but some nitrogen.

DRIED ANIMAL MANURE is available in various types. We use dried chicken manure, which doesn't smell. Animal manures contain only a trace of the major nutrients, but a full range of the trace elements, needed in only very small quantities.

DRIED BLOOD is a fast acting nitrogenous fertiliser, ideal for when plants need a quick boost during the summer.

FISH MEAL contains nitrogen and phosphorus.

HOOF AND HORN contains nitrogen in slow-release form, which is suitable for sustained growth.

LIQUID ANIMAL MANURE contains a small amount of the three major nutrients, plus a full range of trace elements. Make your own health food drink for plants by dunking a cloth bag filled with manure into a bucket of water until it turns the colour of strong tea. Dilute this with four times as much water and use to water vegetables or tomatoes growing in the ground.

LIQUID SEAWEED AND NETTLES contains nitrogen and potassium, but little phosphorus. It's good for supplying trace elements and some growth hormones. A similar cocktail can be made at home with nettle heads. Tie them in a cloth bag, as for the manure above, and when brewed, dilute as above. This makes a high-nitrogen feed for salad crops and herbs.

SEAWEED MEAL contains all the major nutrients plus many trace elements. It is best applied as a good all-round fertiliser, when the soil is warm.

WOOD ASH will provide potassium and a small amount of phosphorus. The exact make-up will depend on the woody material burned. If you burn garden waste, be sure that there is no plastic or other man-made material caught up in the pile. We are lucky enough to be able to have regular bonfires through the winter in our garden, so dispose of larger woody hedge clippings and small branches from trees and shrubs, along with perennial weeds that can't be composted or shredded. The ash produced is dug back into the garden at the end of winter. If you are considering having a bonfire, bear in mind the neighbours' washing, their desire to enjoy the fresh air on a nice day and relationships with the people you might choke. There may be local restrictions on bonfires in your area (in France, we are supposed to get

permission from the mayor between May and October).
In winter, also check for wildlife taking shelter in the
bottom of the pile.

COMPOSTING AND MANURE

BULKY MANURES
Garden compost, well-rotted animal manure and bulky
organic materials such as spent mushroom compost
usually only add small amounts of fertiliser to your
garden. They are, however, invaluable in improving the
structure of the soil, its water-holding capacity and the
ability of the soil to retain nutrients applied from other
sources. Obtaining bulky manures in built-up areas can be
difficult and potentially smelly. If you've got a small
house and garden you won't get many bonus points by
having a large smelly heap of horse manure dumped
outside the front door. My dad tried that one once. Not a
popular move! You can do quite a lot though, even in a
small area, by making your own compost. It also helps
with disposal of grass cuttings, vegetable peelings and
garden waste that may, otherwise, be put into the
ordinary dustbin. This waste of resources isn't so bad if
your local council provides 'green bins' for garden
clippings and cardboard. Sadly, too many councils don't
provide this service. Our council has its own compost-
making plant and they recycle vast amounts for use in the
local area. Some councils sell the compost back to
residents for a very reasonable fee, or even give it away
if you transport it yourself.

DIY COMPOST AND BINS
It's almost impossible to have too much garden compost,
so make as much as you can. It doesn't go far when you
spread it out later. You can form a compost heap without
a container, but if you want your heap to look tidy it's
best to buy a bin or make one from wood. Again, before
forking out on an expensive bin at a garden centre,
enquire with the local council. Many have special offers
to encourage new homeowners. Some provide free
wormeries as well. Our daughter found a very cheap
compost bin on the internet quite recently, at a fraction
of the list price. We've used all sorts of containers over

the years, as you can't easily take the bin with you when you move house, so have tried old dustbins, large kitchen waste bins, leaky water butts, random heaps and home-made wooden bins. We've also got a free 'dalek' style bin from the council, which is brilliant. The advantage of this one is that the base is wider than the top, so you can easily lift the whole bin off the heap for redistribution. You can re-site it easily after emptying, if you find a better position, or you want to improve another bit of garden which it stands on. The leaky water butt has the disadvantage of a rim inside the base, where we cut the bottom off. This one has to be turned on its side and encouraged to 'give generously' with a spade or fork. Heavy work! Some of the others we've tried have hatches at the bottom, but they get clogged up with compost, as do box constructions, where you're supposed to fork out the compost by removing the bottom slats. Wooden boxes can be bought as flat-pack kits, or made out of pallets and bits and pieces.

RECIPE FOR COMPOST

- Stand the bin on a level surface where it can rest undisturbed.

- To provide aeration, place twiggy material at the bottom of the heap, then pile on kitchen and garden refuse that will rot down easily. You can add outer leaves, peelings from fruit and vegetables as well as grass cuttings. See page 30.

- Don't put thick prunings in or woody material unless shredded first.

- If you have large amounts of one type of material, such as lawn mowings, add them in layers about 15 cm (6 in) deep, with other material between. Firm down loose material and dampen dry material after adding to the pile.

- Fill the bin to the top, then cover with a layer of soil, put on the lid if you have one, or cover until the ingredients look like soil. This will take from three to eight months, depending on the temperature.

Ideally, if you have room it's worth having two bins — one to fill and one to leave to rot down. This way you are not tempted to add to the heap that is nearly ready to use.

TIPS FOR QUICK COMPOST

• Use a bin as large as possible — this generates more heat and increases the chance of the material rotting down more quickly.

• Keep material moist and be prepared to water in dry weather if necessary.

• Cover the top in wet weather to prevent waterlogging. Let in plenty of air at the base or sides.

• In winter cover with an old carpet or similar cover to keep it warm. Compost takes longer to mature in cold weather.

• Speed up the rotting process by turning over after a few weeks, then putting back the outside material in the middle.

What to use	Don't use
• Annual weeds • Vegetable garden trimmings, e.g. onion tops, tomato plants • Old bedding plants • Soft hedge trimmings • Lawn clippings • Vegetable peelings • Outer leaves of cabbages, cauliflowers • Fruit peelings • Tea leaves and coffee grains • Dead cut flowers	• Cooked vegetables and fruit or eggshells, which encourage rodents • Weeds with seed heads • Roots of perennial weeds • Diseased plants • Tough stems, unless chopped up • Tree prunings or twigs

LEAF MOULD

If you have large, mature deciduous trees around your garden, or in neighbouring areas, you'll probably have mixed feelings when the leaves blow all over your garden. The vast bulk of rotting leaves can be a real pain, blowing around in the autumn. As fast as you've cleared the lawns and paths, the wretched things are back again. If they fall on the lawn, you must clear them, otherwise the leaves will damage the grass as they decay and encourage bacteria that you don't want. On paths they can become very slippery, even though the family might think it's good to shuffle around in them, kicking them all over the place. If they fall on flower beds there is the possibility of encouraging slugs and snails to overwinter at your expense, and also of course, to kill the plants as they rot. There's nothing more frustrating on a windy day than raking leaves into piles, turning round to get a bag to collect them in and seeing them disappear in all directions. Far better to wait until the wind drops.

TECHNOLOGY AND TOOLS

You may be the sort who would rather try a machine for collecting leaves, but don't bother splashing out on a leaf blower/vacuum. It is quite good fun blowing the leaves all over the place but they still need picking up. The model we tried only seems to like sucking up certain types of leaves, and doesn't like them wet at all. This is a major setback in autumn weather, and given the quantities of leaves we clear every year, completely unworkable. A rake is all you need to collect the leaves and then you can turn this annual job into a valuable organic addition to the enrichment of the soil. You can hold the leaves in some netting, supported by posts, although getting the leaf mould out after two years can be a bit tricky. My husband, who hates collecting leaves almost as much as he hates weeding, has come up with a much more satisfying solution.

LEAVE IT TO THE CRANE BAGS

If you've had any sand or ballast delivered by lorry, you may have a crane bag or two to spare. These can be really useful for a variety of purposes, but the best uses we've found are as collectors of leaves and bins for making leaf mould. We use crane bags, each held in place by four posts driven into the ground to support the looped handles. Make sure there are holes in the bottom. When you want to move them you can, with some help, drag the bags to where you want to deposit the leaf mould. Don't be tempted to put leaves in with your compost because they are more fibrous and decompose at different rates. Oak and beech leaves take up to two years to decompose. Others take less time. When the leaves have formed a crumbly, rich, soil-like consistency, use them as a mulch on bare ground or dig into the top layer of soil, where it will improve the structure.

Ideally you will have a row of three bags to use for different years. As the leaves take rather a long time you won't have to mix different 'vintages' and will always have a bag available for collecting the new leaf fall in October. Because they are so light and deep, crane bags make the ideal container to collect the leaves in the first place, especially if it's windy and you have some help to hold the bag open. On your own there might be a problem as you need at least three hands! An alternative to crane bags, especially for smaller quantities, is a supply of black plastic sacks which you can fill and leave in a corner somewhere, out of sight, to rot down.

GREEN MANURE

A green manure crop is a plant grown mainly to enrich the soil. It is a very old method of soil improvement and often has the added bonus of keeping down weeds as well. Green manure is grown on a bare piece of land, allowed to reach a certain stage, then is dug directly back into the soil. The disadvantage of this method in a small garden is fairly obvious, but there are a variety of plants which can be used to benefit other plants or crops. On a large parcel of land grazing rye can be used, sown between September and November. As it grows it uses nutrients which would otherwise be washed out by rain throughout the winter and also blocks other weeds from growing. In the spring the plants can be dug back into the soil. The root systems of the plants can be huge, but as rye is an annual it won't become a weed. The roots will improve the structure of clay soil.

MUSTARD is a more popular, fast-growing plant that can be used for green manure. You can sow it between crops from May to August and it is ready to dig in after four to six weeks. Mustard adds nitrogen to the soil, rather than improving soil structure.

COMFREY has deep roots and large leaves. If growing well the leaves can be harvested four times a year. There are various ways of using these leaves as instant fertiliser.

1 Cut the leaves and leave to wilt for two days. When you dig a trench for potatoes or runner beans, put a 5 cm (2 in) layer in the bottom before planting. You can also put them under tomatoes.

2 Use them as a mulch between vegetables, and around tomatoes and soft fruits which need high levels of potash, e.g. redcurrants, raspberries.

3 Make a liquid feed by putting the comfrey leaves in a bucket, barrel or butt. Weigh the leaves down to press them, and after a few weeks the liquid can be drained off for growing vegetables, diluted one to ten.

4 Add leaves to your existing compost bin.

RECYCLING LAWN TURFS

If you've decided that you don't want all that lawn when you can grow much more interesting plants or delicious vegetables instead, don't just throw the turfs away or kill them with chemicals. Skim off the top 5 cm (2 in) and pile them up in pairs like sandwiches, green sides inwards. Cover with black polythene and store in a quiet corner for the winter. By the following year the grass should have died off and you will have gained some brilliant top soil to add to beds, or to use in containers as compost. You will have saved money on weedkiller and made a lot of worms and other animals and insects very happy in their winter home. We've even had newts move into ours, from the pond. This is another way of giving something back, instead of always taking from the soil bank, and you help our friends, the worms, as well.

Chapter 5

The Right Tools

Resist the temptation to spend lots of money on professional-looking, stainless-steel tools. You can get to work on your garden with a limited set of tools, starting with a spade, a fork, a rake, a trowel and, of course, a watering can.

Choose a sturdy spade for all your digging and for planting trees and shrubs. As you'll be going for the budget option, make sure the spade isn't too heavy or the shaft and handle too long for you: turning over soil is tiring enough without the extra hassle of a weighty spade that you can't handle easily. The same applies to the garden fork you choose to break up soil and to spread organic matter — light but strong enough not to be bent on its first contact with clay or heavy soils.

A rake is particularly useful for smoothing and levelling surfaces quickly and efficiently. You'll be pleasantly surprised how encouraged you feel after a short spell of raking up leaves or gathering up weeds and unwanted stones and soil. Use your rake also to level gravel paths and quickly transform previously dull-looking areas of the garden.

Although you could manage without a trowel (or a hand fork), it is the most efficient tool for planting small plants and for close weeding. It also stops you from plunging your hands into the soil all the time, making your fingernails filthy if you're not using gardening gloves and causing your fingers to ache for hours afterwards!

Last but certainly not least, a reasonably sized watering can is a must. The removable rose is useful when you need to water or liquid feed plants in pots or containers.

SECATEURS, HOES AND WHEELBARROWS
Unless you have inherited a brand new house and virgin garden space, it's most likely you will have some clearing up to do before you can start digging and planting.
A decent pair of sharp secateurs will soon make light work of stubborn cutting and pruning jobs. Be sure, though, to protect yourself with heavy duty gardening gloves before wading into rose beds or prickly shrubs and bramble-covered areas.

There's a wide range of hoes available to save you the back-breaking experience of weeding on all fours. Types include a Dutch hoe, for slicing weeds from their roots just below the surface, a draw hoe for chopping down larger weeds, and two-bladed hoes that cut weeds with both the front and back edges.

If you have a small garden, you probably won't have room for a wheelbarrow, in which case a large builder's bucket or a rubberised, lightweight container will help you to transport weeds, plants and garden waste. For medium-sized to bigger gardens, a wheelbarrow is the ideal labour-saving device for moving around soil, compost, weeds and rubbish. As with other tools, choose a wheelbarrow that is quite strong and as light as possible when it is empty.

LAWNMOWERS

You can easily spend a lot of money on a lawnmower, so if you have got a small garden, think hard about whether you need to have a lawn. If you do have a lawn, choose the appropriate mower, bearing cost and safety features in mind. Ride-on models and heavy duty petrol mowers cost a fortune and aren't necessarily easy to maintain. You can buy cheap hover mowers and lightweight electric rotary mowers that are easy to manœuvre. With both of these, it pays to collect the grass cuttings every time, unless you mow regularly, in which case the clippings will soon disappear into the thatch of the lawn. Always loop the electric cable over your shoulder when using one of these models, to avoid cutting the cable.

PRUNING, TRIMMING AND SHREDDING

If you have heavy duty pruning to do in your garden, you will appreciate the use of long-handled pruners that will see off the branches and woody stems that your secateurs cannot cope with. Extra-long-handled pruners, known as loppers, enable you to take down thin branches without having to perch dangerously on a ladder. Talking of which, think very carefully before climbing up a ladder to trim your hedge using an electric hedge trimmer. It's all too easy to either cut the trailing cable that inevitably gets lost in the hedge right next to you or to overbalance and risk falling while holding a dangerous piece of equipment.

HALF-MOON EDGING TOOL

A half-moon edging tool used against a straight-edged piece of wood, with one foot on the wood to keep it steady and the other pressing down on the tool, will help to give your lawn and beds a clean and neat appearance. Try not to use it too often, though, otherwise your lawn will shrink and your beds will get bigger and bigger!

STRIMMER AND SHREDDERS

For the places around the garden that your lawn-mower can't penetrate, such as the base of fruit trees, brick edges of greenhouses and narrow strips of grass, a nylon-line trimmer or strimmer is the answer.

Once you are well launched into your gardening, you might like to consider recycling a lot of your garden refuse and producing your own mulch. Provided you have a lot of material to shred, such as thin branches with a bit of sap still in them, you could justify spending a fair amount on a shredder. The shredded material can then be added to the compost heap, where it will rot down more easily, or you could store it in bags until it breaks down into garden much that you can spread on beds to keep down weeds and increase the retention of moisture. Take a look at the cost of garden mulch and you'll soon see how you can make up the cost of the shredder.

STORAGE AND MAINTENANCE

Lockable garden stores are neither cheap nor beautiful, so don't rush out and buy one just to have a place to store your tools. If you've got a garage or utility room, you can put up hooks or tool racks on the walls for your spades, forks, rakes and hoes. In order to guarantee that you don't lose your small garden tools in next to no time, it's a good idea to stick coloured tape around the handles. This makes it easy to spot your secateurs and trowels, if you put them down in the grass or in an overgrown area of the garden.

Whichever tools you buy, make sure you look after them and get full value out of them: after use, clean them with a stiff brush or damp cloth to remove soil, then wipe them dry. At the end of the season you can spray them with an aerosol, such as WD40, or oil them, to prevent rusting.

Chapter 6

Basic Design Tips

Designing a new garden or giving the old one a facelift doesn't have to be difficult or daunting. The main thing is that you don't have to do it all at once, like on TV makeover programmes. We moved to a large mature garden 13 years ago and had a five-year plan for renovating worn out fences, jaded, uncut hedges, digging a pond, laying a patio and building pergolas and a greenhouse. Even attacking one major feature a year, it took nearer ten years, and plans changed a lot in that time. When we moved in, our son, then 13, only wanted one thing: a football goal. Fifteen footballs and several panes of glass later we dispensed with the goal, which stood in front of a holly hedge, opposite my first ever greenhouse. Then we dug up the pitch to grow more vegetables.

STAGGERING WORK

Some jobs can be tackled quickly with little cost, whereas others require major work and a great deal of planning, materials and manpower. It makes a lot of sense to stagger the work and expense over several years, unless you're in a real hurry and moving on soon. In that case, why bother?

DECISION TIME

- Ask yourself what you want from your garden.
- How might things change over the next few years?
- Who will use it?
- What do you want to use the garden for?
- Which plants and features do you want to keep?
- What special features should it include?
- How much time do you want to spend gardening?
- How much can you afford to spend?
- Will it be safe for young children, elderly relatives, or even for you?
- How much sun does the garden get? Which way is it facing?

If the answers to most of the above are 'I don't know', then consider waiting until you've tried some of these ideas:
- Visit gardens of family and friends.
- Visit shows and garden centres with demonstration gardens.

- Watch TV makeover programmes to see which bits you like.
- Use a garden design CD-ROM.
- Look at design books for ideas. You don't have to use all of a design, but something might spark off your ideas.

PLANNING

Some people find it hard to visualise 2D and 3D changes and need some help. If you need to explain your ideas to others you will definitely need to get something down on paper. Even though you're not going to tackle the whole garden all at once, begin by measuring the dimensions of your plot, starting from the house. Walking around the garden at different times of the day and, preferably, at different times of the year will give you changing insights into periods of sunlight, shady patches, wet or dry areas. Stand at windows or doorways looking out, as if through a picture frame. Is the 'picture' pleasing? What would you like to see instead?

1 Make a scale drawing: something like 2 cm to represent 1 metre should do. Mark in the compass directions.

2 Mark the house walls, showing windows and doors. Show boundaries and features you plan to keep, such as trees, shed, pond, etc.

3 Lay a sheet of tracing paper over your drawing, or make several copies of your plan to try out different arrangements of borders, paths, or other features. You can make models if you really need to, in order to clarify your thinking.

4 Come up with two or three completely different ideas to kick about and discuss. Take your time; you can't do it all at once, and you'll have to live with the outcome for some time.

5 Prepare lists of materials you will need and get an estimate of the cost. It might help you to make up your mind where to start, or change your plans to suit your budget.

6 Use hosepipes, sand or ropes to define paths, seating areas, beds, etc. in the existing garden.

PATIENCE

Remember, you don't have to do it all at once! If your house or garden is also a building site, don't get carried away and start too soon, while the workmen are still on site. It's not worth the hassle and misery of seeing your newly dug beds or brand new pathways covered in concrete, muck and machinery. It's far better to hold fire for a few weeks, believe me!

Designing a whole, large garden can be overwhelming. Most of our French garden had been levelled to remove a huge derelict pigeon/rabbit shed by a helpful builder in a bulldozer. We had grass seed put down for the first couple of years, just to keep the weeds in check and give us time to decide how to use the space. This has saved a considerable amount of time and money, because plans for refurbishing outbuildings changed (when they fell down) into the construction of a swimming pool instead. For a gardener, this has been totally frustrating, because the challenge of starting new planting with different soil and climate conditions is an exciting one, and waiting for successive seasons for structural work to be completed has been unbearable. Now, finally, the boundaries are secure, pergolas and fencing for climbers are in place, and tree and hedge planting can proceed.

FRONT GARDENS

If you have a back garden you are unlikely to spend much time at the front of the house, where you are open to view from every passer-by. What you want is something that is easy to maintain and in keeping with the character of the house or neighbouring area. You won't win many friends by being over dramatic with planting or design, or for example filling the plot with garden gnomes and babbling brook. In fact you might generate the unwelcome attraction of others who don't share your sense of style or humour!

Another aspect to consider is deliveries to the house. Stepping stones or a windy narrow path up to the front door might look attractive, but have pity on the postman or delivery drivers, and if you don't want footprints or bike tracks across your new lawn all winter, provide a proper path. The shortest route is a straight line, and human nature drives us all to take short cuts at times. Old pathways or gaps in hedges need to be firmly blocked to prevent visitors, welcome or not, continuing to use your flower bed as a stepping area.

Using screens of shrubs to prevent people looking straight into your living room can be useful, but beware of fast-growing varieties that need regular pruning, or you'll find it getting very dark and gloomy before evening.
If these shrubs are deciduous, you'll have a bit of a problem in the winter, and if the dreaded evergreen *leylandii* is used as a fast-growing fix, you'll be sorry sooner rather than later. See page 53 for some much better suggestions.

TRICKS OF THE TRADE

MYSTERY
You obviously want to be able to look out on to attractive views from the house, but don't plan for everything to be on show from the same place. You want people to go outside and explore.

LONG GARDENS
Make the most of a long, narrow garden by dividing it up into several 'rooms', using trellis, planting shrubs, small hedges or trees. Each area can then have its own character or function, and make visitors curious enough to want to visit the end of the garden. Another trick is to create a curved path which touches both sides of the garden, giving an illusion of width.

SLOPING GARDENS
You can terrace part of a sloping site to make a series of mini gardens leading into each other. If the slope is steep and the area small, make wide steps which can be used to show off pots as well as provide access to lower down. These steps don't have to be complicated engineering achievements. Railway sleepers and gravel are a lot easier than using concrete and bricks. Alternatively, if

space permits, a ramp with wide hairpin bend can provide gentle access for wheelchairs, prams, wheelbarrows, etc.

MULTI-PURPOSE GARDENS

Family gardens should have plenty of grass for summer, paving for winter play, barbecues and sunning yourselves (when you're not busy gardening), borders of resilient shrubs that grow back quickly and don't have thorns or sharp leaves. Avoid fragile or fussy flowers or anything poisonous. Some very popular plants have poisonous seeds, so be careful and check the list on page 158. Play areas such as sandpits can be planned with restyling in mind as the children grow out of them (not as soon as you think!) when they can be turned into planting beds. Ponds must be securely covered and supervised when young children are around.

DON'T

Plan to put a pond close to a large overshadowing tree, which will drop its leaves all over the pond in autumn.

Chapter 7

Hard Surfaces

Although it's reasonable to think that the plants make any garden, hard surfaces, including walls, paths and paved areas, often have an equally important role in adding to the overall visual impact. From a practical viewpoint, too, it's essential to make all parts of the garden easily accessible, both for gardening and for viewing, so be prepared to do some work on hard surfaces. First of all, however, give it plenty of thought, as these permanent features provide lots of hard work and eat up a lot of cash. If you don't like the finished result, you've got a long time to regret your choice!

LOW WALLS

Even low walls need footings: to build a boundary wall of four or five courses of bricks at the end of a patio or paved area, you'll need to dig a trench of about 30 cm. Next, drop in 13 cm of hardcore, broken up and tamped down with a club hammer or sledge-hammer.

Give yourself a level for the top of the concrete using pegs lined up and checked with a spirit level. Pour about 15 cm of concrete in and level off with the pegs and a piece of wood, to tamp and remove pockets of air.

After a few days, when the concrete has hardened off, lay the first course of bricks on a bed of mortar along the top of the footings. At each end of the wall and every 10 to 12 bricks, build small piers/pairs of bricks, alternating them crossways and lengthways, to add strength to the wall and make it more attractive.

PAVING SLABS

You can, of course, use concrete to lay pathways through your garden, but it is not necessarily less work or much cheaper than other, more attractive alternatives, such as paving slabs. These are available in a variety of sizes, shapes and colours. Another advantage of using slabs is that if you lay them on sand instead of cement, you can always move them at a later date if your plans change, or your family needs change. You'll have to weed the cracks and expect some movement when soil dries out, but if the area isn't under constant heavy use, this may be a viable alternative.

As with walls, paving slab paths and patios need a decent foundation: up to 10 cm of hardcore generally for walking on and wheeling barrows over, increasing to 15 cm if vehicles are likely to be driven over the slabs.

Dig a trench deep enough to allow for your broken up and tamped hardcore plus the layer of mortar and the thickness of each paving slab. Use a mixture of one part cement to five parts sharp sand for the mortar.

BRICK PAVING

Using bricks, or a combination of bricks and paving slabs, can add considerably to the appeal of pathways and hardstanding areas in your garden. Chances are you may also have in your garden old bricks that you can recycle, making the job more environmentally friendly and, of course, much cheaper!

Lay several rows of bricks in the pattern of your choice, for example interlocking 'L' shapes or herringbone. Press them gently into a bed of mortar and tamp them down level, using the end of the handle of your club hammer to tap along the length of a straight piece of wood.

Fill the joints with a dry mix of mortar, brushing it into the gaps and pressing down between the edges of the bricks with a small piece of wood to remove pockets of air. Using a watering can fitted with a rose, gently moisten the joints. Use a damp cloth to clean off any excess mortar and mortar stains from the brick surface before they dry.

CRAZY PAVING

Apart from being cheaper because you can use a mixture of paving materials (we even managed to recycle three or four tonnes of local, high street paving that the council sold and delivered quite cheaply!), crazy paving gives your garden a more natural, rustic look. It's also more interesting to lay, as you have several possibilities each time you lay a piece of paving, depending on the effect you want to create.

Save yourself a lot of time and backtracking by laying the pieces dry first of all. Change round as many pieces as you like until you feel the area looks balanced and attractive.

Always start with the bigger pieces, to give you the frame for the area as a whole, and make sure the pieces with straight edges are used to form the sides of your paving. Fill in the remaining gaps with smaller pieces, bearing in mind that you will be mortaring around these pieces, too, so one or two pieces can easily 'fill' what looks like a huge gap between two, three or four big pieces.

When you are happy with the dry arrangement of your crazy paving, bed the pieces in turn on a five parts sharp sand to one part cement mortar mix. As always, use the spirit level to ensure your surface is even. Tamp the pieces individually with the handle of the hammer and collectively using a piece of straight timber across several pieces of slab.

Last but not least, mortar between the joints using your small pointing trowel.

PAVERS AND STEPPING STONES
CLAY OR CONCRETE PAVERS give yet another look to hard surfaces. Although they look like bricks, they are thinner and are designed to fit closely together without mortar joints. That means a lot less back-breaking cement mixing!

Once you have prepared your hardcore base of 5–10 cm depth, you should lay a firm edge to the area, using special edging or concrete edging, bedded on mortar. Check that the edges are level then lay down a 5 cm base of sand.

Fit the pavers together, butting them up first against the edging and then against each other, making sure that they are level across the whole area. Adjust the level of the sand base, if necessary, using a straight-edged piece of wood as a sweeper.

Tamp the pavers down into the sand base, using the club hammer handle end, as before, but this time tapping on a length of timber across a wide area of pavers. For a more professional (and, therefore, more expensive) finish, hire a flat-plate vibrator to do the same job.

STEPPING STONES instead of a path across a lawn save a lot of time, effort and money. They also draw the eye naturally from one part of the garden to another area or focal point, adding considerably to the depth and visual appeal of the garden as a whole.

To lay them quickly and successfully, first pace out in normal strides the stretch of lawn to be crossed. Lay the stones on top of the grass, at the end point of each of your strides. Before continuing, make sure you are happy with the overall look of the stones, especially if your line across the lawn is not meant to be straight.

Next, using a spade or a half-moon edger, cut tightly around the edge of each stone, to a depth a little greater than the stone itself. This is to ensure that it does not stick up above the surface and risk damaging a lawnmower or causing anyone to trip.

Now you can slice out the shape of the stone beneath the grass and lift out the turf. Add as much sand as is necessary, to level the base and keep the stone at the right depth, just below the surrounding grass. Lay the stones in place and check that they are even, using the spirit level.

GRAVEL, PEA BEACH AND PEBBLE SURFACES

All hard surfaces can look too severe in the midst of luxuriant greenery, flowers and plants. It's worthwhile, therefore, considering other materials that come into the category of hard surfaces but have a softening effect.

Don't be afraid to experiment, in order to achieve quite surprising effects with relatively small amounts of gravel, pea beach and beach pebbles.

It doesn't cost a great deal to lay a gravel or pea beach surface next to a path or patio area, whether or not you decide to stand potted plants on the gravel. A gravel path under a pergola leading to a pond, to a flower bed or quite simply to a different area of the garden can look stunning and feels different underfoot.

You can break up the harsh look of paving slabs just as easily, by interspersing them with stretches of pea beach or gravel. You can also create interesting textures and effects using bigger pebbles from the beach bedded in mortar between slabs or courses of bricks, either on a path or in a wall. As always, though, make sure you tamp down the tops of the pebbles, using a solid piece of straight-edged wood, to keep them flush with the rest of the path or area.

DECKING

You can create a completely different effect in your garden by using decking for patios or hard areas. There is a wide range of durable, non-slip decking available with a choice of patterns, usually on double-sided boards.

As with all other hard areas you lay down in your garden, you will need to make sure the area is well supported, preferably on low brick or concrete pads that keep the decking well clear of contact with the soil. Cover the soil underneath the decking with weed suppressing material that allows water but not light to pass through it. If necessary, put gravel down to hold the material in place before you build your decking above it.

Screw or bolt the joists to the pads then lay the decking boards across them, so that you can pre-drill holes to attach the boards. It's always best to screw the boards rather than nail them down, in case you later have to take any boards up for any reason — screws are easier to take out and avoid splitting the wood.

For the sake of safety and of visual appeal, leave a small drainage gap between each of the boards, and make sure all screw or nail heads are countersunk, to avoid injury to hands and bare feet.

Chapter 8

Boundaries

TO FENCE OR TO HEDGE?

It is likely that you will want or have to mark the boundaries of your garden, for security or a more decorative garden, or both. The quickest solution is obviously to erect a fence — it is immediate and you can always start to grow a hedge or plants up against it, once it is in position.

Cheaper fencing, as you would expect, is often quite stark and definitely not decorative. Besides, planting hedging is not only the cheaper, if longer-term option, it is also much friendlier to the environment than building great fences of sawn wood daubed in preservatives that are potentially harmful to plants and animals.

FENCES

INTERWOVEN PANELS

Interwoven panels fastened to posts are the cheapest way to enclose your garden with a wooden fence. They are also straightforward to erect: you can drive the supporting posts into the ground and cement them in. Once the posts are firmly in place, the panels can be nailed to them, preferably using simple panel brackets.

Protect them with a timber preservative that is not harmful to animals and, if you have any plants growing nearby, cover them with plastic sheets or large rolls of fabric to avoid splashing. You will need to treat the fence every couple of years, preferably in the winter when the early plants are dormant and the perennials are still underground. Have some consideration for your neighbours if you choose a bright or contrasting colour for your side of the fence: it may ruin their planting effects by 'bleeding' through a clashing colour, or damaging their unprotected plants. A word with the neighbours first can prevent all sorts of horrors later on!

Apart from being less environmentally friendly, fences such as these also have the disadvantage of not lasting a great length of time. As the panels are generally thin, they soon become brittle and break quite easily. If your garden is situated in a windy site they can become like sails, picking up the wind and rattling all night in a storm. That's if they don't take off!

PICKET FENCES

Picket fences, with alternating wooden uprights and gaps, are more attractive and durable and once again they are not difficult to put up. Unfortunately, being much more substantial, they inevitably cost quite a bit more.

HURDLES

Hurdles, made from long strips of woven hazel, are obviously more natural and are also very easy to install, as there's no need to cement in the posts they are attached to. They have a distinctive, rustic look and add pattern and texture to the garden, wherever they are put up. Don't expect them to be cheap, though!

TRELLIS PANELS

Trellis panels are certainly cheaper than hurdles and are just as easily nailed to posts or even attached to the tops of existing walls, to give your garden greater privacy. They are, though, much flimsier, and really need to be used as a frame for climbing plants, which will also make them a stronger structure for your boundary.

WIRE NETTING

Last but not least, wire netting probably provides the cheapest solution and gives you the opportunity to keep your reputation as an environmentally friendly gardener. How? Simple: once you have tacked your wire netting to posts, plant a hedge just inside it, using common hedging plants such as beech, hawthorn or hornbeam seedlings, which you can buy cheaply in bundles in the winter. Alternatively you can plant a border of mixed shrubs, preferably some that are evergreen, to give all round interest and privacy.

The wire fence shelters and protects your hedging plants as well as enclosing the garden. Then, when the plants are big and strong enough, you can take down the wire fencing altogether, if you wish. Alternatively, you could let the hedge grow through the fencing, making it a much stronger structure that will repel all invaders, including people, pets and livestock!

HEDGES

Provided you are prepared to be patient, planting hedges will, in the long run, bring you greater satisfaction and will cost less. Your hedge will be not only a tough, practical boundary but also an important aspect of your garden, and not just round the edge of the garden. Small internal hedges, to enclose or define, for example, herb gardens or beds, make the garden much more interesting by giving it distinct areas like rooms in a house.
Hawthorn or holly hedges are particularly effective and attractive in country areas where there might be sheep or cattle grazing nearby. At the same time, if you want to attract as much wildlife to your garden as possible, you could consider a mixed country hedge of blackthorn, holly, hazel, elder, dog rose, hawthorn and *acer campestre*: just watch the birds, butterflies and insects enjoying the habitat you have set up for them!

Rosa rugosa hedging is a good idea if you live in an area where it is particularly windy. Remember, a hedge, as well as providing security, also shelters and protects plants from damaging winds that can at worst break them and in general dry them out and cause harmful loss of water.

If you want a neat but substantial country hedge for clipping, you can't do better than beech or hornbeam. For gardeners living near the sea, try clipped *escallonia macrantha* or *hippophae rhamnoides* also known as sea buckthorn. If you need to keep animals or intruders at bay, plant a prickly hedge of berberis or pyracantha or species roses.

Box, laurel or yew will give you formal, evergreen hedging, while dwarf box is ideal for dwarf hedges, as are lavender, hebe, santolina and rosemary.

If you prefer a flowering hedge, try forsythia, shrub roses or *prunus cistera*.

Last but by no means least, the common privet, in its green, golden and variegated forms, provides evergreen, all-purpose, substantial and cost-effective hedging for all types of gardens and situations.

A word of caution for anyone tempted to plant *leylandii*: don't, unless you are prepared to devote lots of time and energy to ensuring it doesn't grow into a giant, impenetrable monstrosity that your neighbours (and you yourself) will hate! It will take over completely and block out the light from other plants. When you chop off the top few metres the trees don't do the decent thing and bush out: they just look awful.

PLANTING A HEDGE

Keep your costs down by buying common hedging plants that are available in bunches with bare roots in the winter. Look for beech, hawthorn or hornbeam seedlings. If necessary, leave the roots to soak for a couple of hours in water, if the plants have been out of the soil for a while. In any event, aim to plant within 24 hours.

Once you have dug your trench, 30 cm deep and wide, add generous amounts of compost and fork it well into the base of the trench. Then sprinkle in some general purpose fertiliser and mix it with the compost. Place the hedging plants about 30 cm apart in a double row, making sure the second row is staggered, forming an elongated 'W' shape along the trench.

Cut the plants back to a height of 5 cm after planting, then water them and mulch them well. It will encourage lots of healthy growth in the first season if you feed and water the plants regularly.

CARE AND MAINTENANCE

A BIT OFF THE TOP, SIR?

The best way to guarantee thick, healthy growth from top to bottom of a formal hedge is to trim the new plants lightly each time they grow 5 cm. If you're looking for a more ornamental hedge or you want quicker results, go for potted bushy shrubs with lots of growth at the base. Plant them in single rows, whenever the soil is workable. To produce a taller, more stable hedge, plant in staggered, double rows, using plants such as laurel or escallonia.

OR SHORT BACK AND SIDES?

Clipping hedges is not as easy as you might think, so follow these suggestions, to ensure safe trimming, a straight line and a cut that promotes continuing growth.

Wear goggles to protect your eyes and thick gardening gloves if the hedge is prickly and use a line attached between two posts, one at either end of the hedge, to give you a level.

The sides of the hedge should be clipped so that the top ends up slightly narrower than the base. This makes the hedge more stable and lets more light and rain get to the roots, keeping the base green instead of dying off.

Above all, beware of trailing power cables that can so easily 'disappear' in the foliage, only for you to 'unearth' them with your hedge trimmer! If you don't have a circuit breaker (RCD) fitted for your electrical gardening equipment, think long and hard before using power tools with cables, such as hedge trimmers, lawnmowers and nylon-line strimmers.

HEDGE YOUR BETS

You can sidestep all of the dangers listed above, as well as most of the work, if you plant a screen instead of a hedge. Try planting a row of bamboo canes or any tight growing evergreen or small, upright-growing trees. They will provide you with an impressive barrier that can also enhance the look of your garden. Make sure first that you know how high they are likely to grow, to avoid the kinds of problems associated with rampant *leylandii*.

A further alternative to exhausting work on a hedge is to use evergreen climbers. Providing you train them along wire netting or a chain-link fence, these climbers will end up concealing the mesh, without growing any higher than the netting or fencing supporting them. See page 87 for more details.

Chapter 9

Rustic Arches and Pergolas

PERGOLAS

A pergola is a series of connecting arches that not only links areas of the garden, it also provides shade and support for climbing plants and a very pleasing way of framing a view or aspect of your garden. Although you can construct a pergola from natural stone, brick, metal or wood, the rustic, wooden version is probably the commonest and the most cost-effective.

An arch or pergola made from rustic timber is relatively simple to construct and is sure to look good with climbing plants. Leave the bark on or use peeled wood: it doesn't matter. If the bark is stripped there will be fewer hiding places for insects, however, and the wood is easier to work with. Rustic poles can be used to make an attractive support for climbing and rambling roses, as well as arches and pergolas. The same basic joints (see below) are used throughout.

A pergola must also be built to dimensions and designs that suit your garden, so plan it on paper first. Perspective is very important too, especially if your garden is on a slope, so get some friends or helpers to hold the poles in position before you start work. That way you can see from a number of different angles how well (or badly!) your pergola will fit in the setting you have chosen.

The easiest way to fix the horizontal poles to the uprights is to make a V-shaped notch in the top of each upright that will cradle snugly the horizontal pole. For a long pergola you will need to join the horizontal poles together. Make sure that all joints occur over an upright pole, to provide strong support. The top end of the horizontal pole sitting snugly in the notched upright should be cut into an L-shape. The adjoining horizontal pole that continues the line should also be cut into an opposing and matching L-

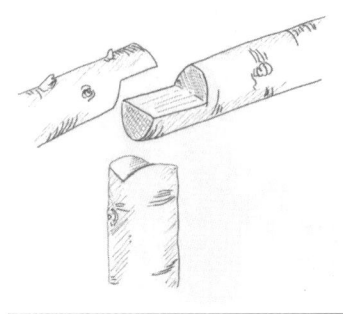

shape, then you can nail them and the top of the upright together with rustproof nails.

Last but not least, the cross-poles should be notched and nailed over the horizontals, to complete the structure. For best effect, allow an overhang of about 15 cm (6 in) on all cross-poles and horizontals.

RUSTIC ARCHES

Once again you should sketch your design on paper before you set about sawing up your timbers. As before, get someone to hold the poles in position first, to give you a chance to see if you have the right height, design and perspective to suit your garden. Remember to allow about 60 cm (about 2 ft) extra on the uprights to sink into the ground.

It's safest and easiest, once you are happy with the design and dimensions, to assemble and erect the sides first (see notes on joints below). When the sides are assembled, drive the uprights firmly into the ground, using a post rammer or a sledgehammer, carefully avoiding splitting the tops of the poles. Alternatively, insert the uprights in ready prepared holes and hold them in position with wooden struts, until they are fully secure in concrete or cement. Check the levels frequently to make sure your structure is at right-angles.

Next, assemble the top of the arch on the ground before attempting to fit it in position. When it is ready, lift it and drill and screw it into position, as nailing it is likely to leave you with too much movement on the structure as a whole.

You can have fun deciding on which basic joints to use, such as V-notches and opposing and matching L-shapes, to fix horizontals to uprights securely and attractively. If you have two crosspieces intersecting,

join them with halving joints, using a saw and chisel to hollow out the joints.

Wood glue will certainly help to strengthen the joints but make sure at least that you nail each joint with rustproof nails.

If you want to be even more technical, you could use bird's mouth joints to connect horizontal or diagonal pieces to uprights. Mark the position carefully, then cut out a V-shape about 2.5 cm (1 in) deep. Saw the joining piece to fit then drive a nail diagonally through the joint. Don't worry if you 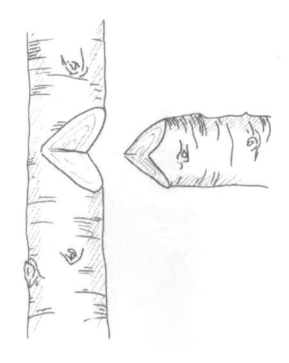 don't get the joints right first time — trial and error is inevitable!

CUT TIMBER PERGOLAS AND ARCHES

If your garden is neither 'cottagey' nor rustic in look and feel, you may prefer the cleaner, more modern lines of a prepared timber pergola or arch. The main difference, in terms of construction, is that there are fewer or no joints, as the horizontals or side rails and the cross-poles or rails are screwed and nailed in position.

As they provide the main support, the side rails are fixed securely to the face, not on top of the uprights, preferably with coach bolts or screws. Where the side rails meet there is no need to cut joints — simply butt the ends of the rails together and screw them to the post.

The cross-rails should be nailed diagonally down into the side rails.

Chapter 10

Making a Pond

Ponds are ideal for encouraging lots of wildlife into your garden as well as adding significantly to the overall visual appeal. They are a great source of interest and education, particularly for children. However, since they can also represent a danger to the safety of very young children, it may be worth while considering instead another type of water feature, such as a pebble pool.

A PREFORMED POOL

Old-fashioned concrete ponds used to be difficult to construct, but with modern liners and preformed pools, making a pond is a job you can complete in a weekend.

1. Place the preformed pool on level ground, then insert canes around the edge and lay a piece of rope around them to transfer the outline to the ground.

2. Excavate the hole, following the profile of the pond and its shelves as accurately as you can. Take measurements and lay the pond in the hole from time to time to check the fit. Don't be afraid to make the hole a few centimetres (inches) larger all round than the actual pond, as this will make backfilling easier later.

3. If you need to check that the depth is correct, lay a piece of wood across the top edges of the excavation, making sure it is level, then measure down from this. If the soil is very stony, excavate an extra 5 cm (2 in) and line it with that depth of sand.

4. Place the pool in the excavation and check that it is absolutely level in all directions.

5. Run water into the pond and, as the level rises, pack fine soil around the edge. If you synchronise the filling with the packing, you are unlikely to disturb the levels.

6. Be sure to pack soil firmly beneath the shelves to avoid causing stresses within the moulding. Use a piece of wood to ram the soil into place if necessary. The backfilling may push the pool upwards, so check the level frequently as you fill and pack.

MARGINAL SHELVES

Although most waterlilies prefer the deeper water in the centre of the pool, the majority of aquatic plants grow in shallow water. A marginal shelf will enable you to grow many kinds of plants.

A LINER POND

1. Mark out the shape of your pond, using a length of rope or a hosepipe. If doing the job in winter, run some hot water through the hose first to make it supple.

2. Dig out the soil to the required depth and barrow it away unless you want to make a raised rock garden behind the pond. Leave a shallow ledge about 23 cm (9 in) wide about halfway down the total depth of the pool. Remove grass from around the edge to allow for the paving which will be used to produce a neat edge. Make this shelf deep enough for the thickness of the paving plus a bed of mortar.

3. Make sure the edge of the pond is level. Space short wooden pegs 90 cm—1.2 m (3—4 ft) apart around the edge of the pool, and go around the pool with a spirit-level.

4. Make sure there are no sharp stones or thick roots sticking out of the soil, then place a cushion of about 12 mm ($^1/_2$ in) of sand on the bottom and the marginal shelves — also along the sides if possible (if you slope the sides slightly and use damp sand it should adhere). If the soil is very stony, use a polyester mat instead of sand. You can buy special matting designed for the job from water garden specialists. To save money and a trip to the tip, you could even use an old carpet to line the bottom and sides of the pond, instead of sand!

5. Drape the liner loosely in the excavation, making sure that there is sufficient overlap all around. Hold the edges in place with a few bricks. Run in water from a hosepipe.

6. Lift the bricks from around the edge and allow the liner to move a little from time to time as the pond fills up with water. There will inevitably be some creases. Remove the worst of them by stretching and adjusting the liner as it fills.

7. Once the pond has been filled to its final level, cut off the surplus liner, leaving a flap of about 15 cm (6 in) all the way round. This will be covered and held in place by the mortar and paving.

8. Bed a paved edge on a mortar bed of three parts sand to one part cement. Rectangular paving slabs are the easiest to use for a rectangular pond, but you can use crazypaving for an irregular shape.

Use this formula to avoid either spending too much money by buying a bigger liner than you need or finding to your horror that the liner is too small for your excavation:

CALCULATING LINER SIZE FOR A POND

- LENGTH OF LINER = LENGTH OF POND + DEPTH OF POND x 2
- WIDTH OF LINER = WIDTH OF POND + DEPTH OF POND x 2
- Allow for some wastage in creases and overlaps

Example:

LENGTH OF POND = 6 metres + DEPTH OF POND = 1 metre, so:

$$7 \times 2 = 14 \text{ metres}$$

WIDTH OF POND = 2 metres + DEPTH OF POND – 1 metre, so:

$$3 \times 2 = 6 \text{ metres}$$

Allowance for wastage, etc. .... =   1 metre

Total .... =   21 sq. metres

A PEBBLE POOL

A pebble pool is perfect for anyone with a tiny garden or small children. It's also ideal for anyone who is too busy to look after a water feature that needs regular upkeep as there is no standing water, just a low, bubbling fountain that runs away through the surrounding pebbles. You get all the sparkle, sound and water movement without the routine work or risks of a pond. They can be landscaped to suit more traditional or even wilder styles of garden, just by altering the surroundings.

HOW A PEBBLE POOL WORKS

Water is endlessly recycled from the fountain into the reservoir. Clean it out once a year and refill it with fresh water.

A perforated lid holds the weight of the pebbles. Because the water is kept in the dark most of the time, it will not become green as it would in a pond. The top of the water pipe coming up from the pump produces a low, chunky bubble of water that will not blow around in the wind.

Pebbles are not provided with the kit, buy them in bags from garden centres for landscaping. Don't take them from the beach. A small pump is all you need to power a simple pebble pool.

ELECTRICAL SAFETY

A lot of people are worried about having electrical wiring in the garden, especially where it is used in connection with water. If you're in any doubt about handling electrical appliances such as these, ask a qualified electrician to install the wiring and pump for you.

INSTALLING THE PEBBLE POOL

Dig a hole deep and wide enough to hold the reservoir. Line the hole with fine sand to cushion the reservoir and the pump. Once you have sunk the reservoir into the hole and made sure it is level, sit the pump in the middle of it.

Fit the perforated lid on the reservoir and over the pump outlet, that should stick out through the hole in the centre of the lid. Fill the reservoir with water and turn on the pump to check that all the water returns to the reservoir. If water splashes over the sides, adjust the pump to reduce the height of the spray. Conceal the lid of the reservoir under a layer of decorative pebbles.

Surround the pebble pool with suitable plants such as hostas and ferns, making sure you dig in plenty of organic matter and keep the soil around the pool well watered.

A bell jet fitted to the top of the pump outlet can produce an attractive spray effect, but you should make sure the breeze does not spoil the shape of the spray effect, by choosing a sufficiently sheltered location for the pool. You will also need to keep the water in the reservoir topped up regularly, as there is inevitable water loss through evaporation.

Chapter 11

Greenhouses and Cold Frames

A GREENHOUSE: TO BUY OR NOT TO BUY?

Unless you're lucky enough to have moved into a house with a greenhouse already in place in the garden (or on an allotment), it's worthwhile pondering the pros and cons of buying one. You need to consider, apart from the cost, the maintenance required, especially if you choose a wooden-framed greenhouse rather than the relatively maintenance-free aluminium models available.

Propagating your own plants and growing plants from seed can be really rewarding and exciting, but you will have to put in a lot of time, effort and money, in order to site and maintain the greenhouse properly.
Costs include:

- *CONSTRUCTION*
- *VENTILATION*
- *INSULATION*
- *STORAGE*
- *SHELVING ARRANGEMENTS*
- *SECURITY*

You will also have to thoroughly clean out your greenhouse at the start of each growing season, to eliminate bacteria, mildew and insects.

On a more encouraging note, if you do go for a greenhouse, you will get well ahead with propagation and planting, and will increase your yield of earlier, fresh vegetables, fruit and flowers. You might even allow yourself a few moments of smugness, when you show off your home-grown peppers, tomatoes, exotic fruits and plants!

COLD FRAMES

Cold frames are invaluable for overwintering vulnerable plants, if you do not have a greenhouse — and, of course, they're infinitely cheaper. Even greenhouse owners find them useful for hardening off seedlings before planting out.

You can either buy cold frames in kit form or build your own. Traditionally, they are made with wooden, aluminium or even brick-walled frames.

Aluminium frames are usually glazed all the way to the ground, so they let in the maximum of light, essential for sturdy growth. Unfortunately, this also means that the frames lose heat quickly through the glass sides, so you will need to insulate them in winter if you want to carry on using them successfully.

Wooden frames are not quite so readily available in kit form, but are popular because they blend in with the garden surroundings better than aluminium frames. If you build your own, go for a simple structure with at least two removable, window-shaped covers that are heavy enough to resist the wind but not likely to give you a hernia when you have to lift or slide them off. Brick-walled frames are, of course, harder and more expensive to construct, but they can look very attractive and the solid structure gives much greater protection to plants than thin-walled frames.

INSULATION AND VENTILATION

If you need to give your plants more protection in winter and you have an aluminium and glass cold frame, insulate the sides with expanded polystyrene tiles. Cut the tiles to a snug size for fitting inside the frame. If you cut the tiles too small and they are loose inside the frame, use card wedged in at one end to hold them in position.

Never insulate the top of a frame permanently, unless you use bubblewrap, because plants need as much light as they can get. When very cold nights are forecast, cover the top of the frame with old carpet or other warm, insulating material. Make sure you do this before the temperature drops too low and remove the cover the following morning, unless the temperature remains low.

In warm weather (and sometimes in winter) good ventilation is vital. Frames with sliding tops come into their own here, as they limit the plants' exposure to potential wind damage.

If your lifting tops do not have an adjustable opening device, make your own wedge from a simple piece of wood. Cut two or three notches into it, to allow you to open the top by increasing amounts as your plants gradually harden off.

Chapter 12

The Right Plants for the Right Place

The art of good gardening lies in knowing what to plant where. It's quite easy to find out what individual plants need — for example sun or shade, damp or well drained soil — if you buy plants from a garden centre, as you'll find information on the back of the label. It's harder to see the growing conditions in different parts of your garden from a plant's point of view, so you may need to do a bit of detective work. The effort will be worth it in the long run as the plants will look after themselves, you won't be playing 'Musical Shrubs' every year like some people I know, and you'll save a lot of money, too.

People may say you need green fingers to be a gardener, but there's no great mystery to matching the plant to the right place. It makes sense to start with easy plants and leave the trickier ones for another year, until you've had some practice and success, otherwise you might be put off.

The first thing to do is to assess your growing conditions, which may vary between one part of the garden and another. You need to establish your soil type and pH of the soil. See pages 12–16.

Next, the general conditions need consideration.
Is the garden . . .
• Shady and damp?
• Open and dry?
• Sheltered and sunny?
• Hot and dry?

• Do you live in a mild or cold region?

• Do you live on a slope, with a frost hollow at the bottom, where frost stays on the ground most of the day in winter?

• From which direction does the garden receive most of its light?

• If on a slope, which direction does the slope face?

• How many hours of sunlight does the garden, or any part of it, receive? One to two hours? Half the day? The whole day?

• How healthy are the weeds that are growing? Weeds are a good way of telling how fertile the soil is. If you have tall strong nettles, there's probably plenty of nitrogen. If weeds are weak and stunted, the soil is poor, and if they are big, leafy and fast growing, the soil is probably quite fertile.

Look at the colour of the soil, compared with surrounding fields etc. If the soil is darker, this shows that it has been well cultivated over the years and contains plenty of organic matter.

MAPPING THE AREA

In a large garden, you can have all of these conditions to deal with. It might help to draw a plan, mark in north and south and use colours to shade areas that are fully shaded, e.g. near buildings, dappled in shade, receiving sun for half a day, or all day. Then you can see at a glance the conditions you are dealing with, and you can take the plan with you when buying the plants and deciding what to grow.

EASY DOES IT

Most popular garden plants are very easy going and will grow in a wide range of sites and conditions, so you don't have to worry about it in most cases, when using widely available plants. It's only when the plants are more expensive or harder to come by that you need to be extra careful. The vast majority of perennial flowers will be happy in a situation where they get direct sunlight for at least half the day. Plants that enjoy similar conditions naturally look right together, which makes it much easier to plan a good-looking garden. Slightly more difficult to organise is the succession of plants which will keep your garden looking good all year round, rather than for three- or four-week bursts in spring and summer. Read on for further advice.

SPECIFIC CONDITIONS

PLANTS WHICH ENJOY CHALKY SOIL
SHRUBS: buddleia, flowering cherry, crab apple, forsythia, hardy fuchsia, phlomis, potentilla
PERENNIALS: gypsophila, pinks, scabious

CLAY SOIL
SHRUBS: berberis, cornus, corylus, miscanthus, roses, salix, hydrangea
PERENNIALS: bluebells, celandines, daffodils, iris

LIME-FREE (ACID) SOIL
SHRUBS: camellia, rhododendron, pieris, heathers, magnolia, azalea

PLANTS FOR AN EXPOSED, WINDY GARDEN
Berberis, birch, chaenomeles, cotoneaster, hawthorn, heather, mountain ash (rowan)

PLANTS FOR A WALL FACING THE SUN
CLIMBERS: campsis, passionflower, grapevine, climbing roses
FRUIT: apricots, figs, nectarines, peaches (slightly tender, needing protection from frost)
WALL SHRUBS: ceanothus, pineapple broom, fremontodendron

PLANTS FOR A WALL FACING AWAY FROM THE SUN
CLIMBERS: ivy, clematis 'Nelly Moser', climbing rose 'Danse du Feu'
WALL SHRUBS: camellia, *Cotoneaster horizontalis*, euonymus, climbing hydrangea, winter jasmine.

DAMP, SHADY GARDEN
FOLIAGE PLANTS: hosta, gunnera, hardy ferns

GARDEN WITH SUN LATER IN THE DAY
CLIMBERS: clematis
CONTAINERS: begonias, fuchsias, petunias
SHRUBS: camellia, quince

GARDEN WITH SUN IN THE MORNING
CLIMBERS: late-flowering clematis, honeysuckle, jasmine
SHRUBS: cotoneaster, kerria, pyracantha

GARDEN WITH SUN ALL DAY
CLIMBERS: grapevine, climbing roses
HERBS: bay, lavender, rosemary, sage, thyme
PERENNIALS: acanthus, achillea, alstroemeria, artemisia, eryngium

ROCK PLANTS: sedum, sempervivium
SHRUBS: buddleia, broom, genista, hebe, myrtle.

IMPROVING YOUR EXISTING PLANTS AND MAKING THE MOST OF WHAT YOU'VE ALREADY GOT

Don't assume that plants will automatically grow into an attractive shape all on their own. Left to grow naturally, some kinds often get themselves into quite a mess. Fortunately, there are lots of ways to improve on nature.

PRUNING A LOPSIDED SHRUB
Remove branches that spoil the shape, cutting them off close to the base of the plant or where they join the main stem. When new shoots start to grow, leave those that balance up the shape and are growing in the right direction and cut off any that lean the wrong way. Don't start pruning shrubs when there is likely to be a frost due, or the plants may not recover.

RENOVATING AN OLD SHRUB
When old shrubs become unproductive and tatty or woody, with little new growth, cut out two or three of the oldest branches as close to the ground or base of the plant as you can. Do this in spring and repeat each year with different branches until all the old ones have been replaced by vigorous new ones. Don't cut back the whole shrub in one go as it may take the plant years to flower again and you'll probably get fed up with waiting.

STOPPING
This is done to make young plants and newly potted cuttings get bushier. Nip out the growing tip of a shoot, using finger and thumbnail. This will make the plant produce several sideshoots at the end of the stem. If you want a big, bushy plant, wait until the sideshoots are 5 cm (2 in) long, then nip out their tips so that these, in turn, grow sideshoots. It took me years to have the courage to do this to plants, because it delays the flowering by several weeks each time to do it and it seemed a shame to nip off the growing tips, wasting even small parts of healthy plants. You can always try planting

the nipped off shoots as cuttings. This is best done early in the season (see later tips).

CLIPPING AND TRIMMING

To maintain the shape of topiary, cloud-trimmed conifers, climbers trained over arches and pergolas you need to trim regularly. Small shears or kitchen scissors are the best tools for small plants. Slow growing plants such as box need trimming twice a year, but faster growing varieties, such as *Lonicera nitida*, may need tidying up every six weeks or so throughout the summer.

RIGHT PLACE, WRONG PLANT

It's tempting to keep cutting back a fast growing shrub that blocks a path or overhangs a step, but all this does is encourage more growth, often without flowers. In this case, it's better to remove the plant entirely and replace with something smaller that won't become a nuisance. You could try replanting the offending shrub, if you can remove it with the roots fairly intact.

PINCHING OUT

You can control the finished shape of plants by pinching out tips of shoots to make them bushier, or by removing sideshoots altogether while they are small. This is very useful for plants whose natural tendency is to grow a few long stems, such as fuchsia, when you want one to turn them into a standard. These look like lollipops.

BUYING NEW PLANTS

Before buying, give any plant a quick once-over. You will soon see that some plants in a section are better than others. In a garden centre, for instance, take a plant away from its group and stand it on the path so that you can look at the whole plant. If it is already showing signs of stress or weakness one side, try another of the batch. Check the label to see how big the plant will grow, and the soil conditions and situation preferred.

It's quite a good idea to buy woody plants, such as trees, shrubs or climbers, when they are in flower. As well as being able to check they are really what they say they are on the label, you can make sure you have bought a free-flowering strain. Some are not as good as others. As long as they are growing in pots, you don't disturb the roots when you plant them out and you remember to keep them well watered afterwards, they'll be fine.

CHECK OUT THE FOLLOWING

• *THE NAME* If the plant is in flower, does it look like the picture on the label? If not in flower and it looks different from the rest of the batch, it may have been wrongly labelled. Check also that it doesn't belong in another section, and has been put back in the wrong place by another customer.

• *BEST VARIETIES* If not familiar with particular plants, always choose varieties that have been given awards. Look for symbols on the label, and if in doubt, ask a salesperson.

• *HEALTH AND CONDITION* Orange spots, black or brown leaves may indicate disease. Broken stems and leaves may indicate rough or careless handling, which in turn may mean that plants haven't been well cared for. Weeds, moss or liverwort growing in the pot is a sign that the plants have been in stock a long time and may need feeding. Poor quality plants can be improved in time, but why spend good money on inferior goods, which will need more care? Choose healthy, vigorous ones that will look good from the minute you plant them.

• *SHAPE* A badly shaped plant can be improved but takes time and patient pruning. If there is no alternative but to buy a lopsided plant, or it's such a bargain and you want a challenge, be prepared to miss a season's flowering. I'm a sucker for bargains and plants that need a bit of TLC, but, believe me, it will be time-consuming and not always result in a rewarding shrub.

WHAT TO LOOK FOR IN TREES

Look for a single trunk with no branches for about 60 cm (24 in) from the ground for a bush tree, 90 cm (36 in) for a half-standard and 120 cm (48 in) for a full standard.

A young tree may have 'feathers' growing out from the trunk. Cut these off, leaving a straight stem up to the crown, where the branches spread out. Look for five or more strong stems branching out evenly all round. A tree with only a few branches on one side will always look lopsided.

WHAT TO LOOK FOR IN SHRUBS

Choose shrubs with five or more shoots growing out evenly from the base. Poorly shaped shrubs are much easier to correct than trees, but you will still lose a season's growth. Avoid shrubs where there seem to be two different types of shoots growing from the same plant, as these will be grafted plants where some suckers are growing from the rootstock. Unless regularly removed, suckers will take over from the plant you really wanted. Roses are a good example of this. Check also that the variety you have chosen is the right size for the space you have. I can think of several examples of friends and family who have unwittingly bought original varieties of plants instead of dwarf varieties.

PLANTING CORRECTLY

It doesn't take long to plant things properly and it's worth doing as it plays such an important part in getting new plants off to a good start. Hurried planting or inadequate soil preparation can mean that plants don't grow well and stay small for years in a sort of suspended animation. It's not unknown for people to leave the pots on the plants when they put them in the ground!

TIMING
HARDY PLANTS
Although you can plant potgrown shrubs at any time of the year when the soil is workable, the best planting times are: mid-spring and early autumn for conifers and evergreens, autumn for woody trees, shrubs, fruit and climbers, spring for hardy perennials and rock plants.

FROST-TENDER PLANTS
Tender plants include slightly tender perennials and shrubs. Many of these are even more tender when they are young. Half-hardy annuals or summer bedding and patio plants are not frost proof, neither are tender herbs like basil and vegetables, including tomatoes, courgettes

and peppers. Watch the weather and don't plant these until just after the last frost in early summer. If you've recently moved to the area, keen gardeners will know when this is likely to be, so ask them or wait and see when they plant out.

HARDENING OFF

If you buy tender plants, before the last frost make sure you can stand them somewhere safe such as a greenhouse, cold frame, carport or sunroom. Harden them off for 10 to 14 days to accustom them gradually to outdoor conditions. During the day, stand them outside and bring them in at night. If you have a cold frame you can save yourself effort by just taking the lid off during the day (see page 66 for more on cold frames). Watch out for slugs and snails during this period, which will be looking for a tasty, tender leaf salad or two to chomp. If you don't have somewhere to harden off plants, it's a good idea to leave them in the garden centre until after the frosts. Once bedding plants are displayed outdoors there, you can be pretty sure that it is safe to plant them out.

SOIL PREPARATION

Don't skimp on your soil preparation. If you skipped the section on groundwork on page 12, do not pass go! Don't plant until you've prepared properly. If possible, prepare the ground in the autumn and leave it rough through the winter, so that the birds can clear up the soil pests for you. Fork it over to turn up those pests still hiding underground. If you are planting a whole new bed, spread a thin layer of well-rotted organic matter (did you read about the importance of compost, page 28?) over the surface. Fork over the ground, removing any weeds and roots as you go and turning in the compost. Rake the ground roughly level, removing any stones or roots. If you are preparing for seed sowing, rake extra well, leaving it looking like cake crumbs. If you are planting a single shrub, spend as much time digging the hole as you did choosing the plant. Dig a big hole, mixing in plenty of compost and fertiliser unless you're planting in autumn or winter.

PLANTING DEPTH

As a general rule put in plants so that the top of the rootball is level with the surrounding soil. Exceptions to this rule are bearded irises, where the top half of the rhizome should be above the ground after planting. Clematis need to be planted deeply, with the top of the rootball 10—15 cm (4—6 in) down so that they can send out new shoots from underground stems if they are damaged by careless weeding or clematis wilt disease.

PLANTING A TREE

When you plant a tree, hammer in a short stake alongside at an angle of about 45 degrees, with the tip about 30 cm (12 in) from the base of the tree. That way, there is no risk of the tip impaling the rootball. Fix the trunk to the stake using a proper tree tie. Always tie the tree to the stake, not the stake to the tree. Be sure to water thoroughly. This washes the soil down around the roots so that they are surrounded by soil and not air pockets. Trees planted in the autumn normally need less watering, as the weather does it for you. If you plant in the spring you'll need to water throughout the summer.

Chapter 13

Planning a Mixed Border for Interest All Year Round

Mixed borders contain a bit of everything — trees, shrubs, roses, evergreens, flowers and bulbs — so that they remain colourful all year round. You need quite a large area to fit in so many different plants, but in a small garden you can make a smaller mixed border without the trees and use only small shrubs. One way of planning the border is to cut out pictures in catalogues to see what the plants look like with various companions. Another way is to photograph groups of plants which take your fancy in other gardens. When buying plants, try arranging them in groups before you buy. Some of the most successful border combinations, however, come about by pure accident, and it's not always the colour-coordinated, tapestry effects that give the 'wow' factor. When planning a border, try to choose plants that will give interest at different times of year. The best ones are those that have more than one attribute, for example new growth colour and spring flowers, or summer flowers and autumn leaf colour. Alternatively, choose some plants for the different seasons, for example bulbs for spring interest planted with summer flowering perennials.

ALTERNATIVE BORDERS

You don't have to choose a traditional mixed border. By varying the mixture of plants used, you can create a particular style to suit your taste. Here are some suggestions.

HERBACEOUS BORDER

A traditional blend of summer-flowering perennials, such as delphiniums, gypsophila, lupins, phlox and stachys. Traditional herbaceous borders are less popular in modern gardens than they used to be, but you can grow them imaginatively. Herbaceous borders don't have to be too polite. Tall plants growing in groups make a striking display against a brick wall or a backdrop of evergreen shrubs, which works well, even in a small garden. The advantage of using perennials is that once you've bought or acquired the plants you don't have to restock every year, and as the plants spread, they provide good ground cover to keep down the weeds. Some perennials, such as *Geranium endressi*, die down in the winter. If you want evergreen cover, try bergenias or epimediums. If possible, leave a narrow access path along the back of the border.

SUBTROPICAL BORDER
Tender or exotic-looking plants, such as canna, dahlias, castor oil plant, gazania, phygelius and shrubby salvias. Tropical beds are very showy; but most of the plants aren't hardy. This means that you will need somewhere safe to keep them throughout the winter to protect them from frost damage.

COTTAGE GARDEN BORDER
Old-fashioned flowers (including hardy annuals such as nasturtiums), herbs, campanula, Canterbury bells, foxgloves, lavender, roses, sweet williams. In a cottage-style border small spreading and self-seeding plants such as diascia, eschscholzia, geranium and nepeta, are encouraged to grow into each other to create a colourful tapestry that looks good, even in a small garden. This is a money-saving border, where saved seeds can be used for annuals.

ROSE BORDER
Standard, bush, compact and patio roses with contrasting underplanting of foliage or flowers. The problem with rose beds is that you don't get all round colour from the roses, which are the main feature.

ANATOMY OF A BORDER

TALLEST AT THE BACK, PLEASE
When planning your side bed, obviously the taller plants need to be nearer the back as a general rule. There are some exceptions, where tall, fine-leaved or delicate plants such as grasses can look good in front of more dense shrubs or perennials. Traditional beds have the very tallest centre back, with successively shorter plants to create a tiered effect. Stand in the area you are going to plant and think of the plants' heights compared with your height.

• *SHOULDER HIGH AND ABOVE* Choose standard trees that have a bare trunk to at least 1.2–1.5 m (4–5 ft), so that the crown is raised well up above smaller plants.
• *WAIST TO SHOULDER HEIGHT* Choose shrubs with a mixture of foliage colours (including variegated leaves), different flowering times and naturally tidy shapes that will slot in under trees. A sprinkling of evergreens provides winter interest, but don't go overboard. Shrubs that tolerate

light shade are best for planting right underneath trees.

• *KNEE TO WAIST HIGH — HERBACEOUS FLOWERS* Choose kinds that are happy to grow in light shade, because at various times of day they will be in dappled shade cast by bigger plants. This means all but the real sunlovers.

• *ANKLE TO KNEE HIGH — ANNUALS AND CARPETING PLANTS* Choose plants that naturally sprawl or make low compact mounds to fill gaps in the bottom floor of the border between other plants. Alternatively, grow masses of spring bulbs to give the same effect early in the year before perennials have grown up again.

WHAT SHAPE OF BORDER?

A TRADITIONAL BORDER
This runs round the edge of the garden, just in front of a wall, fence or hedge; it is usually quite wide. A formal border has a straight edge, an informal border has a curved one that looks much more natural. Traditional borders help to define the shape of the garden. With tall trees or shrubs around the edge of the garden, it is more sheltered and private. On the down side they can be a lot of work, as weeds grow through from the garden next door, and plants get drawn up by lack of light at the back of the border. This means that you will need to stake many of the plants to keep them upright.

ISLAND BEDS
These go in the middle of a lawn, where you can see them from all round. They are less work because plants grow shorter and stronger due to the better light. Only the tallest will need staking. The beds are easier to weed because you can get at them from all round but they take up more room in a small garden, and can make mowing more of a faff.

NARROW BORDERS
These can run along either side of a path, or along the edge of a feature such as a patio. Keep to smaller plants here, or the garden will start to look closed in and oppressive. They help to shape the garden and add colour and interest, but too many small borders can make a garden look fussy and create a lot of extra work.

Chapter 14

All About Perennials

Perennials are flowers that die down in the autumn and spend winter as underground roots but reappear each spring. They were traditionally used as the mainstay of herbaceous borders, but nowadays are frequently grown as single plants in containers as well as in stylish borders. Perennials are a varied group of plants and there are some to suit all situations around the garden.

YEARLY CYCLE OF CARE		
Season	**Signs of Life**	**Action Required**
Spring	New shoots start to appear through the soil.	Weed, feed and mulch. Cut back more tender varieties.
Summer	Most perennials in flower.	Deadhead regularly.
Autumn	Foliage starts to turn yellow.	Cut back to just above ground level, or leave until spring if needing protection.
Winter	Deadish appearance above ground.	Leave alone! Dormant, not dead.

EASY-GOING PERENNIALS

Here are a few popular perennials to try. A more comprehensive list can be found on page 157.

CROCOSMIA

Once called montbretia, they have lance-shaped leaves and flower all summer. They grow from underground corms, which build up on each other year by year. They like sunny, well drained positions, but they seem to grow anywhere and everywhere. Once established, they will happily fill the whole bed and can become rather too invasive. They make a nice splash of colour on a patch of land next to our garden, where they were dumped years ago, so are fairly unfussy. The flowers are orange to red and produced on double, tubular ranks. They are excellent for cut flowers. *Crocosmia Star of the East* is a popular variety.

ACHILLEA

This has flat-topped clusters of flowers all summer.
These contrast well with spike-shaped perennials, like
crocosmia. *Achillea Coronation Gold* is yellow, or if you
prefer pink, try *A. Smiling Queen*.

MICHAELMAS DAISIES

These are vigorous, tough perennials, which won't need
much attention once established, other than containing
their expansion across the border. They are part of the
Aster family, a genus of 500 species, ranging in height,
flower size and colour.

SCABIOUS FLOWERS

Excellent for cutting, they grow in any well drained,
sunny site. They will need staking or they flop about.
Easily grown from seed, they self-set, if allowed.

LYCHNIS

Lychnis species which are hardy perennials include
Lychnis coronaria. They are not long living perennials, but
self seed generously, providing hundreds of seedlings
which you can transplant to other areas. The stems are
greyish and slightly furry and the flowers are a rich
magenta, which can look stunning with the right colour
scheme.

LAVENDER

Lavenders can be used in a variety of settings, providing
low hedging, have fragrant flowers and aromatic foliage.
They are great when planted alongside a path or drive,
where people will brush against them. They grow leggy
with age and should be replaced every five years or so.
A wide range of varieties, including 'butterfly' types is
widely available and can be grown from seed.

PRIMULA

Primula varieties are an asset to any garden, being hardy
and often flowering very early in spring. From the
ordinary primrose-like *Primula vulgaris* (Polyanthus)
varieties to the more spectacular *P. auricular*, they are
fairly easy to grow providing the soil is not too dry in
spring or summer.

EVERGREEN PERENNIALS

A few perennials are evergreen, so won't die down but will stay green all winter. They are especially valuable in small gardens, or where they are constantly on show, because they don't leave empty spaces in winter. Examples are:

BERGENIA
An easy-to-grow — anywhere plant with 'elephant's ear'-shaped leaves and late spring flowers. The leaves of some varieties turn red or purple in autumn and winter.

DIANTHUS (pinks)
The grey-green foliage is attractive in winter. There are several species which form cushion-like growth.

EUPHORBIAS (some)
The flowers of many euphorbias are insignificant, but the leaves provide interest. *Euphorbia robbiae* has dark green, leathery leaves and thrives in shade. *Euphorbia Wulfenii* is a bushy evergreen shrub with spearlike leaves.

HELLEBORES
These are invaluable for a small garden. Not only are they evergreen, they flower in early spring, before the majority of perennials.

HEUCHERA
One of my current favourites. There is a wide range of species which are ideal for edging borders or for providing ground cover under trees. They also provide decorative cut flowers in a range of red and pink and some varieties have beautiful bronze or chocolaty foliage. Bonus!

BOG GARDEN PERENNIALS

The way to turn a problem wet spot into an attractive bed is to plant naturally damp-loving plants together. Most also grow in normal borders that never dry out badly. When preparing the soil for moisture-loving plants, dig in plenty of well-rotted organic matter which will hold water and mulch in the spring.

ASTILBE are classic plants for damp to boggy soil. There are plenty of white, pink, red and magenta forms to choose from.

CALTHA (marsh marigolds) are equally at home in a bog garden or in a container standing in water. Our pond has a thriving colony growing in the shallow water on the marginal shelf.

GUNNERA vary in size from dwarf varieties reaching 10 cm (4 in) to 2–3 m (6–10 ft), so be careful which ones you pick! The giant varieties have enormous dark green kidney-shaped leaves.

HOSTA are grown for their foliage and heads of nodding trumpet-like flowers. They are at home in shady areas as well as in woodland and waterside areas. Consider their use in containers (see below), especially if you have a slug problem.

LYTHRUM, or cultivated forms of the wild purple loosestrife, are colourful and won't spread and take over.

PRIMULA Varieties such as *P. pulverulenta* have striking tiered flowers and look good with hostas. Most primulas tolerate damp conditions.

RODGERSIA are grown as much for their foliage as their flowers. Different varieties give white, pink or red flowers.

Ferns make up a large group of plants, most of which grow in tropical areas. Hardy ferns, however, make great foils for flowering plants and grow very well in moist conditions.

PERENNIALS IN CONTAINERS

If you don't want to bother replanting annuals each season, consider growing specimen perennials instead. This method isn't exactly low maintenance, though, and you'll need to water regularly. Container perennials do have the advantage of being mobile, if the pots aren't too big. It also means that in a small garden, on a patio, or even on a balcony, you can have brilliant displays which you move around as the whim takes you. Pests such as slugs and snails are given a run for their money, too. I've been known to grow dahlias, lupins and delphiniums this way as well, to defeat the dreaded beasts, but these plants need some support.

Choose compact kinds with a long flowering season or good foliage. Plant in late spring, using a strong frost-proof container and soil-based potting compost. You can add slow release food, if you want to. Water regularly from mid-spring to early autumn. When deciduous varieties die down cut the tops off, as for ground-grown varieties. In winter keep the containers outside, but raised up on bricks, or without trays underneath, to prevent waterlogging. If they are close to a wall, check that they don't dry out. In more prolonged spells of cold weather you may need to move the tubs or insulate them. This will prevent the potting mixture from freezing and killing the plant or cracking the pot.

HERE ARE A FEW SUGGESTIONS
• Hosta. As above, these are really impressive in plain terracotta pots. As they are especially yummy to slugs and snails, the best way to keep them from being eaten is in pots. Try smearing plant-protecting jelly round the pots to make a complete barrier. Standing the pots in gravel will also help, as slugs don't like gritty surfaces.
• Most grasses make good container plants although some will die back in winter. Evergreens are good all year, so don't cut them back. Try *Festuca glauca*, *Carex comans*, or *Carex 'Evergold'*.

CLIMBING PERENNIALS

You can be creative with climbers and make good use of walls, fences and trellis, arches, pergolas and obelisks. If you want a speedy screen to make a garden more private, growing climbers can provide a quick fix. There's more information on climbing roses in Chapter 20.

Think before you plant
  •Don't plant self-clinging climbers like ivy or Virginia creeper onto house walls with crumbling mortar or

render, as they will make the damage worse. Ivy demolished our 1 m (3 ft) thick, garden wall in France, and grew through the stone wall of the house!

- Avoid plants like wisteria in a small garden, otherwise they will take over and require constant pruning. The stems become very thick and strong, so don't let them climb around drainpipes or over gutters, which will eventually be liberated from the wall.
- If buying clematis, check which variety you have before pruning, as you may not need to prune it at all.

Here are some popular climbers to try:

CLEMATIS
Large-flowered hybrids, such as 'Nelly Moser', have large saucer-shaped flowers in summer. A variety of colours is available. Roots like to be kept cool, but the tops like the sun. Grow them through trees as well as on trellis or pergolas.

Alpine varieties have bell-shaped flowers in spring and don't need pruning.

Montana varieties are usually white or pink and flower in early summer. Very good for growing through trees, but on a pergola they can look unsightly after flowering and strangle other plants.

LONICERA (honeysuckle)
Scented summer stranglers. They grow wild in our hedges and trees, so I've relegated them from the pergola, where they fought with the clematis Montana and made a bird's nest construction. Beware the evergreen varieties, which are even more rampant.

VIRGINIA CREEPER and BOSTON IVY
Huge, fast-growing, self-clinging climbers. Brilliant autumn colour guaranteed, but don't put them on the house wall.

WISTERIA
Truly spectacular in the right place, with long, drooping flower racemes in early summer. Traditionally, the lilac/mauve varieties are most popular, but the white ones are equally stylish on a pergola, with white roses.

DIVIDING PERENNIALS

Sooner or later, those perennials chosen for ground cover will need some attention. You may see the middle of a clump dying out, or they may stop flowering so well. Fast growing varieties like Michaelmas daisies will need restraining eventually; probably every three years or so. Others may grow happily for longer. Don't divide until you have to.

Divide plants with fibrous roots, such as Michaelmas daisies, in autumn, with two forks placed back to back. By alternately pressing the forks against each other and then in the opposite direction, you will soon pull the plant apart.

Loosen the clump with a spade or fork and, if it's not too heavy, lift it on to the surface of the soil. Otherwise try to divide it into smaller pieces first.

To keep the plant vigorous and flowering well, leave the pieces large. A large clump will easily divide into six good-sized pieces. Discard the centre of the old plant and replant only the vigorous pieces from around the edge.

PROPAGATION

If you are dividing for propagation purposes, pull the pieces apart by hand into small sections, each with a shoot and root. Pot them up or grow them on in a spare piece of ground until large enough to plant in the border.

Chapter 15

All About Lawns

WHY HAVE A LAWN AT ALL?

Although it is easy to assume — mistakenly — that a lawn does not need any attention once it is established, it is true that it is easier and quicker to maintain than a whole series of beds and borders. It also provides a centrepiece for a garden and, provided it is not neglected, it will enhance the impact of the beds, flowers and shrubs you choose to go around or in it. Laying a lawn also buys you time to plan: once the lawn has been established for some time, you can easily decide to adapt it by adding paths or features or by cutting out beds.

A LAWN FROM SEED

Using seed to grow a lawn is obviously far cheaper than turfing, and if you sow at the right time, it won't take long to become established. Ideally spring or early autumn are the times to sow, but if you have to sow during the summer, make sure you water regularly during bouts of dry weather.

First, drive in some pegs and use a spirit level to ensure they are level. Next rake the soil level to lines 5 cm (2 in) down from the top of the pegs. Now firm the soil, treading it evenly to remove any large air pockets.

Rake the soil to a fine, crumbly structure that will be suitable for sowing seeds. Leave the area for a couple of weeks, to allow weed seedlings to germinate, then hoe them off or kill them off with a chemical weed-killer that is safe enough for you to be able to replant within a few days. Give the ground a final raking before sowing.

Choose a grass seed to suit your purposes. Generally, the mixtures of lawn seed that contain ryegrass are hard-wearing, while those without ryegrass are suitable for high quality decorative lawns that will not be subjected to heavy use.

Divide your sowing area into square metre sections: mark out 1 metre-wide strips with pegs and string, then divide each strip into 1 metre sections. Using a small container as a measure for the amount of seed you need for each 1 metre square section, scatter half the measure in one direction over one-half of the section, then scatter the other half on the rest of the section in the opposite direction.

When all the seed has been sown, lightly rake it into the surface. In dry weather use a lawn sprinkler to prevent the germinating seedlings from drying out.

A LAWN FROM TURF

If you are feeling rich and want instant results, go for a turf lawn instead of sowing seeds. Provided you keep the turfs well watered if the weather is dry and you avoid frozen ground, you can lay a turf lawn more or less whenever you want. Spring and early autumn, though, are still good times to choose for turfing.

Once you have prepared the ground in the same way as you would for sowing seed, lay your first row of turfs against a straight edge, such as a path or low wall. Butt each turf close up against the previous one, to help them knit successfully.

Stagger the remaining rows like brickwork, to avoid long, continuous joints across the lawn. Kneel on a plank to spread your weight along the grass you have already laid. Roll the plank forward as you move from row to row.

Once the turf has been laid, still standing on your plank of wood, tamp the turf down to remove air pockets, using the back of your rake, or roll the grass with a garden roller. Next, brush sieved sandy soil or a mixture of peat and sand into the joints, to further bind the grass together.

If you need to trim the edges, use an edging iron or half-moon edger. Make sure you stand on a plank as you trim, to keep the edge straight.

ROUTINE LAWN CARE

While a well-groomed lawn can set off all the other features in your garden, it is equally true that a neglected lawn can spoil the overall effect. If you remember to feed, weed, brush, trim and aerate your lawn, it will give you good service for many years.

FEED ME!

Feed the lawn once a year with fertilizer. You can spread the fertiliser by hand, as you do for sowing lawn seed (see above), or you can use a mechanical spreader.

WEED ME!

If the lawn is covered in weeds, apply a weedkiller in mid- or late spring. Ideally you should use a watering can with a dribble bar, applying the weed-killer in regular strips to avoid missing any sections or double-dosing.

If you only have a few weeds to get rid of, use spot treatment. Brush or dab on a selective lawn weedkiller, making sure you don't kill off any of the grass next to the weeds.

BRUSH ME!

Keep the lawn clear of debris and worm casts. Although they will not harm the lawn directly, they could provide seed beds for weeds to grow in.

TRIM ME!

Trim the lawn edges periodically, preferably using a nylon-line strimmer with a swivel head. Otherwise, the heavier (but cheaper) long-handled shears will do the job, albeit a lot more slowly.

CHECK MY BALD PATCHES!

Reseed bare patches in the lawn before weeds have the opportunity to fill the space. Loosen the surface first, then sprinkle on a small quantity of grass seed. Water well and protect the patch with a sheet of clear plastic until the seeds germinate.

SPIKE ME!

Remove old clippings, moss and dead grass with a lawn rake, to keep it looking healthy and green. Once you have raked the lawn, aerate it with a fork. Push the prongs in about 15 cm (6 in) deep, in rows about 8–15 cm (3–6 in) apart. Then brush sand into the holes, if your soil is heavy clay. If your soil is sandy, brush peat into the holes instead.

Chapter 16

Trees and Shrubs

Trees are ideal for providing height for the back row of a mixed border. Most small gardens don't have a lot of room for trees, so you must choose carefully. There are plenty of very attractive decorative kinds that won't outgrow their welcome, but if you only have room for one tree, make it a good one. Plant as far away from the house as their eventual height will be.

Don't be tempted to plant a large forest tree such as an oak or beech, or a willow with far-ranging roots. They can cause problems with foundations and drains. If you already have a large specimen oak or beech which you want to remove, or prune radically, check with your local council first, as there may be preservation orders in operation. Felling such a tree can cost you £1,000 in some cases!

Shrubs are woody-stemmed plants that create the basic shape of your garden and are a good choice for a garden that is easy to look after. Once planted there is little to do. There are many types of shrubs available and you can choose them for particular looks to suit your garden. Some small compact shrubs make good container plants for all year interest. Shrubs vary in size from quite small plants, suitable for a rock garden, to huge plants which take up as much room as a tree, so read the label carefully before you buy.

SPECIMEN TREES AS A FOCAL POINT

HERE ARE SOME GOOD TREES FOR SMALL GARDENS:
• *Acer pseudoplatanus 'brilliantissimum'* is very slow growing, achieving 3 m (10 ft) eventually. It has bright, bronzy, salmon-pink maple leaves and is a relative of the sycamore.
• Chinese red birch *Betula albosinensis* is a typical birch, but with spectacular pinky red peeling bark
• Judas tree, *Cercis siliquastrum*, has a craggy appearance, with mauve-pink pea flowers growing straight out of the branches in late spring, followed by kidney-shaped leaves. It needs a mild garden, so is unsuitable for colder regions.
• Crab apples. There are many good varieties, such as

Red Jade, with large spring blossom, followed by small berry-like fruit that attracts the birds in autumn. See below under fruit trees for another use for these trees.
• *Gleditsia triacanthos* 'Rubylace' eventually reaches 4.5 m (15 ft). It has delicate ferny foliage that changes from red in spring to bronze later on.
• *Salix caprea* 'Pendula' or Kilmarnock willow is a small, well-behaved weeping variety that has pussy willows in the spring. It reaches from 1.8 m to 3 m (6–10 ft), depending on the stem it has been grafted to.

TREE CARE

Give your trees a good start in life: after planting make sure that they grow into an attractive and appropriate shape, reduce competition from weeds and protect them from animals.

TRAINING

If you want a multi-stemmed tree or one with branches close to the ground, buy one with shoots along the length of the trunk. Prune out only those that are badly positioned, or crossing other shoots, and allow the others to grow. Shorten the remaining sideshoots to within 5–10 cm (2–4 in) of the trunk. Do this only once.

If you want a tree with a dominant central leading shoot, make sure that it has not developed two leaders – perhaps because the growing tip has been damaged. Prune one of them back to its point of origin, leaving the dominant or most upright leading shoot to continue upward growth.

If you want a tree with a clear trunk, cut back all the new shoots above the branching head to about 10–15 cm (4–6 in) during the summer. When the plant is dormant, cut the shoots right back to the stem.

Some trees – such as crab apples – are best with a rounded, branching head rather than a tall central dominant shoot. Remove the lower shoots to produce a stem, as described above. When the tree has reached about 60 cm (2 ft) taller than the required final height of the clear stem, remove the tip of the leading shoot.

CONSERVING MOISTURE AND CONTROLLING WEEDS

Trees will become established more quickly and grow faster if you ensure that they do not go short of water. Insert a pot close to the roots so that water penetrates to the roots quickly instead of running off the soil's surface.

An organic mulch, such as garden compost, pulverised bark or cocoa shells will conserve moisture, keep down weeds and can look more attractive than bare soil. Make sure that the ground is moist and weed-free before applying it. The layer needs to be at least 5 cm (2 in) thick to be effective.

Although less attractive visually, inorganic mulches are just as effective at keeping down weeds and conserving moisture. You can make the sheet look more attractive by covering it with a layer of gravel.

OTHER THINGS TO CHECK

- Check variegated trees once or twice each summer and remove any all-green shoots. They grow faster than the patterned leaves and eventually take over the plant.

- Don't grow grass right up to the trunk of a tree. You risk damaging the bark when mowing or strimming and ultimately risk killing the tree.

- Protect new trees from rabbits as they will strip the bark in winter. Surround the bottom 90–120 cm (36–48 in) with a special spiral tree guard which has holes for ventilation, or make a collar of wire netting at least 90 cm (36 in) high.

- If you have a big tree in your garden that blocks out the light, don't try to do anything to it yourself. It's a job for a professional, who will have the right equipment and expertise to lift the crown by removing the lowest branches or thin it out to let more light through, without spoiling the shape of the tree. This service doesn't come cheap, but it's a lot safer and prevents a beautiful tree from becoming an eyesore.

- Evergreen trees and shrubs will benefit from wind protection for the first autumn and winter. Fix wind-break netting or a plastic sheet around four canes or stakes, but leave the top open. Remove it in the spring.

FRUIT TREES

You might think that fruit trees take up too much room in a small garden, but nowadays various compact forms are available. You can also train fruit trees into a wide range of space-saving shapes on fences or trellis, which makes them both decorative and productive as wall plants or garden dividers.

SCIENCE
For a crop to 'set', most fruit trees require another variety (and in some cases two) to cross-pollinate them. If there isn't another tree of the same species that flowers at the same time as yours within about 100 metres — maybe in a neighbour's garden — then you'll need to plant one. Consult the nursery or garden centre to see which varieties will cross-pollinate each other. Ornamental crab apples have a long flowering season and cross-pollinate most varieties of apples. 'John Downie' is a good pollinator for apple trees, and has its own crop of rosy crab apples in autumn that are decorative and make excellent crab apple jelly. Otherwise, grow a self-fertile fruit variety, such as 'Greensleeves' apple, 'Conference' pear, 'Victoria' plum or 'Stella' cherry.

FITTING FRUIT TREES INTO A SMALL GARDEN
DWARFING ROOTSTOCKS The most popular fruit tree types are now available growing on dwarfing rootstocks. These keep the trees naturally dwarf and also encourage them to start flowering and fruiting when they are much younger than usual. This means you could plant a fruit tree instead of a flowering tree at the back of a border or as a specimen tree in the lawn, knowing it won't outgrow its welcome.
GENETIC DWARFS Patio peaches and nectarines are available that are naturally small trees producing full-sized fruit. They are ideal for growing in pots on the patio.
CORDON-TRAINED TREES Instead of growing a conventional tree, buy cordon-trained apple or pear trees

(which are grown on dwarfing rootstocks) and grow them against a post-and-wire support as a fruiting 'hedge', or over an arch or fruit tunnel.

FAN-TRAINED TREES You can buy trees of plums, nectarines and peaches trained in a fan shape to grow against a sunny wall. This helps to ripen the fruit, as well as saving space and looking good.

ESPALIER TREES These have one main trunk with two tiers of branches growing out horizontally to make a flat tree. They can be grown against a wall or used as a living 'garden divider'. Pears need warmer conditions than apples to grow well and ripen, so they are a good choice for espalier training against a wall.

FAMILY TREES These have one trunk, but each branch is a different variety of apple chosen to pollinate its neighbours. This way, you can enjoy a range of flavours and be certain of getting a good crop.

SHRUBS

Shrubs form a permanent framework for the garden and help to give it shape throughout the year. If a border formed entirely of shrubs doesn't appeal, used them as part of a mixed border. If you get them off to a good start, they won't need much attention or effort from you, which has got to be a good thing!

BALLED PLANTS

A few plants such as rhododendrons and lilacs may be sold with their roots wrapped in hessian or plastic. These have been lifted from a field. When planting them, prepare the ground as on page 76, remove the root wrapping, but don't disturb the rootball.

CONTAINER-GROWN SHRUBS

If you are planting a new border or group of shrubs, space them out on the ground while they are still in their pots so that you can see what they'll look like. Continue as on page 76.

IMAGINATIVE PLANTING

You can plant a mini border using dwarf shrubs. Choose a mixture of foliage and flowering shrubs, deciduous and evergreen so that there is plenty to look at all year round.

Shrubs with a strong profile or bold shape, such as *Fatsia japonica*, yuccas and phormiums, make good focal points. Use a brightly flowered shrub as a focal point to view across the garden against a background of less colourful shrubs.

Foliage lasts longer than flowers and in a dull corner or shady border yellow leaves or bright lime-green or bronze foliage can be as bright as blooms.

SPACING
After five or ten years, most shrubs increase greatly in size, so don't overcrowd your shrubs initially. Plant the main shrubs with final spacings in mind. Read the labels! Fill in with cheaper, quick growing shrubs that you can dispense with and not feel too guilty about getting rid of.

MOVING AN ESTABLISHED SHRUB
Quite large shrubs can be moved, with care. There are bound to be times when you change your mind, or the dwarf variety you thought you had turns out to be a monster. Move deciduous plants when dormant. Evergreens are best moved in autumn or spring. If the plant has prickly branches, tie them into an upright position to make the job easier.

- First of all, prepare the new hole for the plant you are going to move. Make sure it will be large enough.
- Dig a trench all round the plant then use a fork to loosen the soil around deeper roots. If the shrub is large you may need to reduce the amount of soil attached to the roots with a fork, being careful not to damage the roots at the same time.
- Use a spade to cut underneath the rootball, working around from different sides. If the plant and rootball are heavy, get help.
- Ideally, you want to replant as soon as possible, but if there will be a delay, wrap the rootball in a plastic or hessian sack until you can get it back in the ground.
- Make sure the plant is at the same level as previously. Fill the hole carefully and stamp down the soil to remove air pockets. Water well and continue to water for some time, until growth restarts.

MULTI-PURPOSE SHRUBS

Where space is short, go for reliable, free-flowering plants, especially if they offer the bonus of other attractions later in the year. You need a variety for seasonal colour and a leafy background to your borders. Here are some good suggestions:

CHAENOMELES JAPONICA (ornamental quince)
Spectacular spring flowers are produced in white, pinks and reds, with medium-sized green fruits all summer which ripen to gold in the autumn. They can be slightly untidy shrubs but can be pruned regularly and are a real bonus in a mixed, natural or cottage-style setting.

CORNUS ALBA 'Spaethii'
Cornus give good colour in the winter from red stems, visible after the leaves have fallen. The green and gold variegated leaves of this variety are a bonus.

COTONEASTER HORIZONTALIS
This works equally well as a ground cover shrub or leaning against a wall. Herringbone-shaped fans of foliage keep their tiny leaves in all but the most severe winters. The branches are outlined in orange or red berries in autumn.

FATSIA JAPONICA
Fatsia is a favourite with flower arrangers, who cut single leaves or whole stems to use with cut flowers. This architectural evergreen with big 'fig leaves' flowers in late autumn, when there's not much else going on. You can expect clusters of fluffy, cream-coloured balls.

HAMAMELIS (Witch hazel)
One of my favourite winter and early spring shrubs, it also has good autumn leaf colour. The flowers appear on the bare stems of branches in winter as scented, yellow, orange or red spiders. *H. intermedia* 'Pallida' can grow quite big in time. We have one in the garden that we keep small by pruning. The yellow flowers are just wonderful, and last a long time.

HEBE
Most varieties grow naturally small and compact. These evergreen flowering shrubs are fairly hardy and come in a range of colours from white to blue, pink and purple. They make good, low hedging plants or a border along a path. *Hebe x andersonii* 'Variegata' has a good spread of 60—90 cm (2—3 ft), wavy spearlike foliage in mid-green

and cream. The lavender 'bottlebrush' flowers are seen from July to October. We have many hebes in the garden that we inherited many years ago. Their range of foliage and colour has much to recommend them, and they can be easily propagated to fill gaps and replace old shrubs.

PYRACANTHA

This grows into a big shrub, but we keep ours small by cutting off the new shoots just beyond the clusters of flowers in midsummer. That way, you still get clusters of berries late into winter. The spiny evergreen branches make a good boundary plant to deter intruders but this plant can also be grown up against a wall. Watch out for the spikes!

HIBISCUS SYRIACUS (Hardy hibiscus)

This is a slow-growing, upright shrub with large flowers, similar to the houseplant. If the weather stays fine, hibiscus will flower continuously from midsummer to autumn. They don't need pruning.

PAEONIA SUFFRUTICOSA (Tree peony)

Tree peonies grow slowly and stay as medium-sized shrubs for many years. They need a sheltered spot, otherwise the large tissue-papery flowers are spoilt by the wind. The foliage is good, even when there are no flowers.

CERATOSTIGMA WILLMOTTIANUM (Hardy plumbago)

Suitable for a container, raised bed, or at the front of a border, this dwarf shrub has blue, starry flowers in summer and autumn and good leaf colour in autumn.

WEIGELA

The small, compact *Weigela* 'Florida variegata' has cream and green leaves and clusters of pink flowers in summer. It looks good planted with roses, as the leaves contrast well with them, or is equally good as a specimen plant on an otherwise boring border. *Weigela florida* 'Foliis Purpureis' is good in a border and has plum-purple leaves and deeper pink flowers.

Chapter 17

Annuals

GROWING HARDY ANNUALS

Hardy annuals are charming 'old-fashioned' flowers that are now making quite a comeback. Unlike summer bedding plants (also known as half-hardy annuals) they are surprisingly cold-tolerant, so you can grow your own plants without needing a greenhouse or any special equipment. Just sow the seeds in pots or seed trays in a porch or car port, or straight into the ground in the garden, and move the plants to where you want them to flower when they are big enough to handle easily. Although hardy annuals die off at the end of the season, they often drop seeds in the soil that grow in autumn or the following spring, giving you a supply of new seedlings, which will, hopefully, survive the winter.

Sweet peas are popular hardy annuals for cutting. For the earliest flowers, sow seeds in pots in a cold greenhouse in autumn and plant them out in spring. Alternatively, you can start them off on a windowsill indoors or in a greenhouse in early spring. Just watch that they don't get too leggy.

COTTAGE-STYLE PLANTING

Old cottage gardeners didn't have the time or money to go in for a lot of fancy gardening techniques, so their gardens were the 'take-care-of-itself' variety. You can create the same haphazard effect at home, anywhere you want a border that doesn't need much looking after, so long as it gets the sun for about half the day. Start by planting a selection of cottagey-looking perennials that don't need digging up and dividing, such as lady's mantle (*Alchemilla mollis*), astrantia and campanula. In the soil around them sow poppies, clarkia, viola and godetia. Some of the perennials will spread and some will self-seed. The annuals will also self-seed, so that by year two they all mingle together, cover the ground and flower without you having to do more than lift out the odd weed that doesn't get smothered naturally, and remove any stray seedlings that come up where you don't want them. You might need to restrain some of the more rampant strains of campanula and alchemilla, but it's better than having weeds growing. Red nasturtiums, orange calendula marigolds and bronze-leaved fennel make a good flowering combination for an easy cottage garden effect.

Sow hardy annuals from early to mid-spring. If you keep them regularly watered and deadheaded, you'll have plants in flower for most of the summer.

TO GET GOOD STRONG PLANTS:

1. First make sure the area is weed free, then rake the ground level. Break up any lumps of soil.
2. Water the soil before you sow the seeds so that you don't wash them away.
3. Sow the seed very thinly along a groove or shallow drill in the ground. Space large seeds 5 cm (1—2 in) apart. Take tiny pinches of small seeds and spread like salt along the grooves. If the seeds are really small, mix them with sand before sprinkling so that they don't all land in the same place. You might want to use sand as a guideline for planting as well.
4. Cover lightly with soil.

MASS PRODUCTION

If you want plenty of hardy annuals all round the garden, the quick and easy way to raise large quantities is to borrow a couple of rows in the vegetable garden or an empty flower bed and turn it into a temporary nursery. Fork the soil over well — there is no need to add fertiliser. Scratch a long, straight, shallow groove with the tip of a cane and water using a fine rose on a watering can. Sprinkle the flower seed thinly along it. Barely cover the seed with a fine scattering of sieved soil, and when seedlings appear, wait until they are a manageable size and then thin them out so that they have more room to develop. Once they make bushy young plants 5—7.5 cm (2—3 in) high, dig them up carefully with a hand fork and replant them where you want them to grow. When the seedlings are about 2.5 cm (1 in) high, 'weed' out the smallest ones to leave the strongest spaced 7.5—10 cm apart. Keep them watered in dry weather. Once the plants are 5—7.5 cm (2—3 in) they are ready to be moved to their flowering positions.

SIMPLE SOLUTION

Hardy annuals are the simple solution, if you want to grow summer flowers that you can just sow straight into containers and leave to come up without any pricking out or transplanting. Good choices include naturally compact bushy kinds, such as dwarf nasturtiums. However, given a structure to climb on, self-clinging climbers, such as sweet peas and canary creeper (*Tropaeolum peregrinum*), are very successful sown in hanging baskets or large pots. Short varieties of sunflower are also fun for sowing into good-sized 15–20 cm (6–8 in) diameter terracotta pots. To avoid backache stand the containers where you want the plants to flower.

Hardy annuals don't like over-rich soil, so fill each container with a seed mixture. Nasturtiums are best sown into a mixture used to grow something else the previous summer. They only need poor soil, otherwise they just produce huge leaves and very few flowers. Space out large seeds, such as nasturtiums and sweet peas, 2.5–5 cm (1–2 in) apart, so they have room to grow. When the seedlings come up, carefully pull out the weakest ones, leaving the rest 10–15 cm (4–6 in) apart.

In the case of pots of sunflowers, plant a cluster of three or four seeds in the centre of a pot and push them down into the mixture so they are barely covered. Water well when the seedlings come up. Leave the strongest one and pull out the rest. Keep all young plants watered and begin feeding when they have been growing for four to six weeks, except in the case of nasturtiums.

EASY HARDY ANNUALS

• *ALYSSUM* Low growing, 15 cm (6 in) or under, trail on the ground and produce white, pink or purple flowers.
• *CLARKIA* Showy flowers from 30–50 cm (12–20 in) in salmon pinks, reds, lilacs and purples.
• *CORNFLOWER* (*Centaurea cyanus*) Single or double flowers in red, blue, white and pink, height 90 cm (3 ft).
• *GODETIA* Very easy to grow, height 20–45 cm (8–18 in), papery flowers in pinks, reds and white. Seeds well so we always have some in the borders.
• *CANDYTUFT* (*Iberis umbellata*) has white, pink or

purple flowers on stems 20 cm (8 in) tall.
• *MATTHIOLA BICORNIS* (night-scented stock)
For fragrance on a warm night, pale lilac flowers.
• *NASTURTIUM* (*Tropaeolum majus*) Alaska Mixed is
perfect for a hot-coloured border, with red, yellow and
orange flowers and variegated foliage. Undemanding and
a firm favourite of mine.
• *NIGELLA* (love-in-a-mist) carry circular flowers on stems
up to 60 cm (2 ft) in blue, white and pink. Don't
deadhead, as the huge seed pods are good for drying for
flower arrangements.
• *ESCHSCHOLTZIA* (Californian poppy) Shades of white,
yellow and hot orange on slender stems of 45 cm (18 in).
Also a good self-setter, with pretty foliage.
• *SUNFLOWER* Varieties of giant, dwarf and bushy plants
in red and bronze as well as yellow. Leave the large
heads on the plant after the petals have fallen and you
will get circles of tightly packed seeds that will attract
wild birds to the garden.
• *SWEET PEA* Available as mixed or single colours.
A 'must have' for the scent as well as colour palette.

HALF-HARDY ANNUALS,
OR SUMMER BEDDING PLANTS

These plants are, as the name suggests, not as hardy as
other annuals. If you want to grow them from seed you
really need a greenhouse or a conservatory to start them
off, otherwise the season will be half over before they
begin to grow, let alone flower. Alternative ways of
buying are as plugs or as larger, singly potted plants.
This is the most expensive way, and unless you're not
bothered about the cost, or have only a few tubs or small
beds to fill, the plugs are your best bet.

GROWING SUMMER BEDDING PLANTS FROM PLUGS

Many people opt to buy plugs, especially if they don't
want dozens of indentical plants. These young plants are
growing in multipacks that look rather like egg boxes.
You can buy 'plug plants' by mail order from catalogues
issued in spring by the seed firms and other specialist
plant raisers, and plugs are also available at most good
garden centres. Plug plants are usually small seedlings,

but they are sometimes supplied as tiny rooted cuttings. It doesn't matter, as you treat them both the same way. In order to travel safely by post, mail-order plug plants are supplied with quite substantial packaging. It is vital to take them out of the pack as soon as possible after delivery, even if you don't have time to plant them straightaway.

CARE FOR YOUR TENDER PLANTS

You can't just put delicate patio plants straight outdoors into wind, rain and fluctuating temperatures, when all they've ever known are stable conditions in a greenhouse or indoors. You need to toughen them up first. Start hardening them off two to three weeks before the date you expect the last frost in your area. Other gardeners will know when that is, if you are new to the area. See Chapter 12, page 76 for more information.

If it turns cold, windy or very wet, wait until the conditions improve. If you happen to plant out a bit too soon and a cold night is forecast, then cover containers of tender plants with layers of horticultural fleece or newspaper. It only gives a little frost protection, but that can make the difference between life and death for your tender plants.

PICK OF THE PLUGS

Here are some of the best varieties that will keep your borders, baskets or containers looking colourful from the start of summer right through into autumn. If you only buy small quantities of these you will be able to propagate quite a few of them, with very little effort.

• *SCAEVOLA AEMULA* 'Blue Wonder' is a popular plug plant often used in containers and hanging baskets, although it can also be planted in borders. The flowers are fan-shaped, hence the common name of 'fairy fans'. Stiff horizonal stems make for a good frill round the edge of a tub.
• *PELARGONIUMS*, often wrongly called geraniums, are old favourites, available in a wide range of colours as well as the traditional red. They make good plants for dry conditions and are great for containers as they don't mind if they are left to dry out. Very easy to propagate.

• *CONTINENTAL CASCADING PELARGONIUMS* These are special varieties of trailing ivy-leaved pelargoniums. They have flowers with narrow petals, but in such huge numbers as to smother the plants, which flower profusely all summer.

• *CALIFORNIA DREAMERS* A range of fuchsia varieties with exceptionally large, flamboyant flowers. They need a warm spot to really do well. Unlike other varieties which are hardy shrubs, these need looking after. Fairly easy to propagate.

• *BEGONIA SEMPERFLORENS* These are fibrous-rooted begonias, which are indispensable as bedding plants and container plants. The variety of leaf colour and cascades of flowers from white to red last forever and are a really good plug plant to buy as they are a bit tricky to grow from seed.

• *DIASCIA* Spreading stunner, with short spikes of flower in coral or salmon-pink shades. Good in warm conditions, and with a very long flowering season.

• *PETUNIAS* Surfinia petunias have large, scented, weatherproof flowers on strong cascading plants. One of the best container plants, it keeps flowering vigorously right through the summer. A great plant for dry, hot places. Deadhead frequently for continuous flowering.

• *MILLION BELLS PETUNIAS* have smaller flowers, but masses more of them and are even more weather-resistant.

• *TRAILING SNAPDRAGONS* Grey, furry leaves form a mound of felt-studded white or pink flowers, picked out in lemon. Long flowering season.

• *VERBENA* has become very popular as a hanging basket 'filler' now that it is available cheaply as a plug plant. Use it for contrast between large flowers such as petunia.

• *TRAILING VERBENA* Pretty and free-flowering plants in a range of colours for a more traditional effect. They look really good with deep reddy-purple pelargoniums or with fuchsias. Easy to propagate for a second show later in the season.

CHOOSING YOUR COLOURS

Bedding plants don't have to be bold and brash, boring and predictable or over formal. I would always try to avoid making my garden into a red, white and blue extravaganza of bedding, but each to their own. Try experimenting with shades, contrasting foliage or height in a bed. Predominantly white plantings can look really good with one or two pale lilacs, pansies or silver foliage like cinerarias against a green background. Cool, but not cold is the theme. Informal groupings usually appeal to gardeners like me, who dislike formal, regimented rows. Try two, three or even four different colours and forms interplanted so that they grow into each other. It'll give the weeds something to think about, too!

SPRING BEDDING PLANTS

As soon as summer bedding has finished you can clear and replant for spring. Just when you thought that you had finished with gardening for the year!

PREPARING FOR PLANTING

- Lift the remains of the summer bedding and fork over the ground to get rid of any weeds.

- If you are using plants that you have grown yourself, water well before transplanting. Lift with as much soil as possible and plant with a trowel, making sure that the spacing is right.

- The most common spring bedding plants are wallflowers, forget-me-nots and pansies. If you are using bought wallflowers they are often sold as bare root plants. Plant these as soon as possible to prevent them from drying out.

- If you are planting a mixture of more than one kind of bedding plant check the spacing and layout first, then fully plant a section at a time to prevent the problem of treading on the plants. If you want to interplant bulbs with spring bedding, plant the bulbs as you go so that you don't dig them up by mistake when dealing with the bedding plants.

- A single colour wallflower bed interplanted with tulips looks stunning. Try a rich contrast, such as deep ruby wallflowers and orange tulips, or orange wallflowers and white or black tulips.

Chapter 18

All Sorts of Bulbs

SCIENTIFIC STUFF

Gardeners tend to call any plant with an underground storage organ 'bulb', even when technically it may be a tuber, corm or rhizome. You will find all these types of plant sold as dry 'bulbs' in the same section of the garden centre, and by post in bulb catalogues.

To make the most of a small garden, it is essential to pack in as many plants as possible. Bulbs are especially valuable, as they pop up, flower and then duck underground again. Plant bulbs as the bottom layer of a tiered planting scheme, under shrubs and perennials, so there is always something new coming out in bloom to keep the garden changing throughout the seasons.

A YEAR IN THE LIFE OF A SPRING BULB

- *AUTUMN* Planting time.
- *WINTER* The bulb takes root and in late winter shoots appear above the ground.
- *SPRING* Flowering time. Most of the bulb's energy reserves are used up in producing leaves and flowers, and it shrinks.
- *LATE SPRING* As the flowers finish, the leaves are using sunlight to make carbohydrates that refill the bulb.
- *EARLY SUMMER* Six to eight weeks after flowering, leaves start turning yellow, the bulb is stocked with winter stores and contains a tiny 'bud' that will produce the following year's flowers.
- *SUMMER UNTIL AUTUMN* The bulb is dormant underground, safe from predators (hopefully) and drought.

PLANT SPRING-FLOWERING BULBS IN AUTUMN AND SUMMER-FLOWERING BULBS IN SPRING

SPRING BULBS

Plant late-rooting bulbs, such as tulips and hyacinths, in mid- to late autumn, two months after early-rooting ones such as daffodils, which you can plant as soon as they appear in the shops.

- *DAFFODILS* are the traditional 'first sign of spring', but choose dwarf varieties if you don't like the sight of long floppy foliage for weeks after the flowers are over.
There are many different varieties to suit taste and pocket.

- *CROCUSES* show the true versatility of bulbs. They can be grown in pots, window boxes, beds and borders when there is not much else out and can be naturalised in the lawn or under trees. Unfortunately the birds seem to love pecking at the yellow ones in our garden and many corms seem to get eaten.
- *TULIPS* often succumb to pests and diseases if left in the ground, so are best lifted and stored after flowering. Alternatively, plant in containers (see below).
- *SNOWDROPS* are usually transplanted with their leaves on, immediately after flowering.
- *HYACINTHS* are more commonly grown indoors these days, but they make a stunning display in borders and provide heady scent as well. Plant them 12—15 cm (5—6 in) deep in autumn. Don't expect old, previously forced bulbs to give much of a display though, as they've been treated and the forcing process weakens them considerably.
- *CONVALLARIA* or lily of the valley grow from a creeping rhizome and spread quickly under the right conditions. They are excellent for wild gardens or in shady corners.

THREE THINGS TO REMEMBER WHEN PLANTING BULBS IN BEDS OR BORDERS

1   To make bulbs look as if they grew naturally, drop a handful on the ground and plant them where they fall.

2   Use a trowel or bulb planter to make a hole for each bulb and press the bulb firmly — down into the bottom. Then replace the plug of soil that you removed when making the hole and cover the bulb with it.

3   As a good rule of thumb, plant spring bulbs to three times their own depth.

THREE THINGS NOT TO DO WITH BULBS AFTER FLOWERING

1   Don't cut down the foliage of spring bulbs until at least six weeks after they finish flowering, or they won't flower next year.
2   Don't mow grass where bulbs are naturalised during this time.

3 Don't knot your daffodil foliage either. It doesn't look
   very nice and it stops the leaves doing their job
   properly.

Bulbs lie dormant for much of the year, so if you are new
to the garden, this is another good reason for doing
nothing in a hurry. Leaving them in the ground, once they
are identified, can be a real saving on time and effort.
If you use a stick to identify where they are it might
disappear, or be tidied up by mistake. Try using a pebble
or three to mark the spot. Eventually large clumps of
bulbs will need to be divided and replanted. If you do this
while the foliage is still visible it will be easier to see
where the clumps are.

DEALING WITH PESTS AND BEASTIES

To stop squirrels stealing your flower bulbs, bury a piece of
small-mesh chicken wire 2.5 cm (1 in) below the surface
over the area where the bulbs are growing. This also stops
you slicing into dormant bulbs when you are hoeing

If soil pests are a problem, dust bulbs with pesticide
powder before planting. If mice are your problem, plant
bulbs with a layer of holly leaves over the top. They take
several years to rot.

To avoid new bulbs rotting in damp soil, sit them onto
2.5 cm (1 in) of grit in the bottom of their planting holes
and sprinkle them with yellow sulphur dust.

GROWING BULBS IN CONTAINERS

Growing bulbs in containers not only creates attractive
displays, but also gives you the opportunity to move them
around the garden, and to hide them when they have
flowered, while you are waiting for the foliage to die
down. The other advantage is that with very small bulbs,
such as grape hyacinth and snowdrops, you know where
they are.

If the container is a large one, stand it where you want
the bulbs to flower.
- Put some drainage material in the bottom of the pot
  and cover this with 2.5 cm (1 in) of soil-based potting
  mixture.

- Put in as many bulbs as you can, but don't let them quite touch each other or the sides of the pot. Press them firmly down.
- Cover the bulbs with 2.5 cm (1 in) of potting mix. Repeat with a second layer of bulbs. If the container is deep enough, add a third.
- If the bulbs don't come quite to the top of the mix, plant the top of the container thickly with annuals, such as pansies, so there is something to look at before the bulbs start to flower.
- Water just enough to dampen the potting mixture evenly and check it regularly. Don't overwater but don't let the mix dry out, either.

SUMMER BULBS

HARDY PLANTS

- *LILIES* can be planted in spring or autumn, depending on when bulbs are available, but don't leave them out of the ground for long, as they dislike drying out. Once planted, they are best left undisturbed to build up slowly into bigger clumps. There are about 80 species of lilies and most are quite easy to grow from bulbs. They come in a variety of colours and forms, with a rich scent you either love or hate. Try planting two or three spectacular 'Star Gazers', well supported, in a large pot by a patio door. You will be well rewarded.
- *GLADIOLI* The spear-shaped foliage makes a good foil for bedding plants before the spikes of colourful trumpet-shaped flowers appear in midsummer. Gladioli die down in autumn, but the same corms flower again the following year. Dwarf gladioli make a good show in patio pots for the summer. Plant the corms 3.75 cm (1.5 in) apart in spring and cover them with 2.5 cm (1 in) of potting mixture.
- *AGAPANTHUS* or African lilies grow in compact clumps. When grown in pots, they need to be overcrowded to encourage flowering. The deep blue or white, hyacinth-like flowers like a sunny, sheltered position and don't like being disturbed.
- *ALLIUM* are quite easy to grow, even from seed, if you are the patient type. Forms vary considerably from chives to spectacular pom-poms, which is what you get if you leave onions or leeks to go to seed in the vegetable patch.

I've taken to doing just that, as the flowers are so good.
• *IRIS* varieties fall into three main categories (bearded, beardless and bulbous) and can flower from April through to June. Different types prefer different conditions, with some growing in water. Generally they don't like being disturbed and bearded irises won't flower if you plant them too deep. Plant them with the top half of each tuber above the ground, in a sunny spot.
• *CROCOSMIA* can become a bit too successful, so choose 'Emberglow' for large red flowers or 'Solfatare' for apricot/yellow flowers with bronzy leaves.

NON-HARDY PLANTS
• *CANNAS* are perfect for adding a touch of tropical flair to the borders, but plant canna and tuberous begonia in pots in a heated greenhouse and don't move them outdoors until after the last frost.
• *DAHLIA* tubers are usually planted dry in late spring, but because they are planted 7.5 cm (3 in) deep, there is no risk of the tender shoots appearing above the ground when a frost might nip them off.
• *TIGRIDIA*, which combine the characteristics of tulips and irises, and acidanthera bulbs which have fragrant, star-shaped flowers, are planted in the garden around the time of the last frost, in April or May.

Frost-tender bulbs must be harvested in autumn before the first frost. Dry off the bulbs and store them in a protected place until the next planting time comes round.

PLANTING
As with spring bulbs, plant them approximately three times their own depth. Exceptions are *Lilium candidum*, where the tip of each bulb should show just above the ground, and hardy cyclamen. The tops of their tubers should be just above ground.

AUTUMN BULBS

• *AUTUMN CROCUS* and *COLCHICUMS* are only available for a few weeks in late summer. Plant them straightaway, as they flower within a few weeks. Although they are expensive, once in the ground they can be left alone and will slowly increase naturally, building up colonies.

• *HARDY CYCLAMEN* are planted in late summer and early autumn in well-drained soil. They do best in woodland conditions.

Chapter 19

Herbs

Herbs are handy in the kitchen and fashionable in the garden, and those with an attractive scent are doubly welcome. There is no need to make a separate herb garden, especially if you are short of room. Herbs can be grown in flower beds, in the vegetable garden, or in a pretty 'potager'. Where space is short, most of the popular kinds make good plants for containers. If you cut lightly, you can still use them for cooking or to preserve for winter use.

Even if you're not short of space it can be very useful to have a pot of those herbs you use more frequently by the back door, to avoid a long trek down the garden path in the rain, every time you want a bit of parsley!

Many herbs are leafy and rather dull, and a formal herb garden is a good way to display them. If it has a strong geometric shape it will be a feature even in the winter when most herbs have died down. If you have the space, make it complex and ornate, with formal paths dividing the beds, and perhaps an ornament such as a birdbath or sundial as a centrepiece.

If you do not have space for a formal herb garden, a 'chequer-board' herb garden created by lifting alternate paving stones makes an interesting feature for a large patio, especially if it needs relaying or sprucing up a bit.

MEDITERRANEAN HERBS
Bay, marjoram (oregano), rosemary, sage and thyme are all reasonably hardy sunlovers and need very well-drained, not too-fertile soil and a warm, sheltered, sunny spot. All except marjoram are evergreen, and all grow into small, compact shrubs, except bay, which will eventually make a large tree. Bay is often grown in a pot and trained into a small standard or pyramid shape. Taking cuttings is easy.

Purple sage is as good for cooking as the plain green variety, but adds colour to your border or arrangement. Other varieties of marjoram, e.g. golden marjoram and thyme, also add colour and texture to mixed borders. Thyme grows well in gravel, so placed along a gravel path it will get trodden on at times and give a pleasant scent to the area.

OTHER POPULAR PERENNIAL HERBS

Chives, mint, tarragon and fennel. These are larger plants that can spread — in the case of mint, by runners. Tarragon and chives make clumps that slowly spread, and both chives and fennel self-seed freely. They need moist, fertile soil and sun for at least half the day. They are all hardy.

MINT CONDITION

If you plant mint in the ground, be prepared to do battle at some stage to eradicate it from the bed, and if you try to grow it in a container with other herbs, it will take over. To stop mint spreading, grow it in a leaky bucket or a big flowerpot and sink that almost to its rim in the garden. Plant mint in soil-based potting mixture, but don't fill the bucket quite to the top. Leave a 5 cm (2 in) gap, so that there is a low barrier that stops the mint runners getting out and escaping into the garden. Mint is a greedy plant, so it needs repotting into fresh potting mixture every spring, otherwise it fades away. If you want masses of mint (but why would you?), you might consider using a growing bag to prevent it taking over the world! This way you could grow several varieties like applemint, peppermint, etc. These are quite attractive varieties, but there's a limit to how much mint you want for your new potatoes, and as for mint sauces? Try explaining putting it on roast lamb to a French friend!

DECORATIVE HERBS

Borage, chamomile, lemon verbena, lavender, pinks and scented-leaved pelargoniums. These are prettier than they are genuinely useful — most people only use small amounts — so add one or two to containers to 'pretty up' the greener, culinary herbs. They all need similar conditions to the Mediterranean herbs, except borage, which is an annual. Add them to flower borders or plant them for fragrance close by places where you sit or walk. The blue starry flowers of borage are edible and can be used to decorate salads or buffet tables. Freeze them into ice cubes to liven up summer drinks. Lavender is a traditional herb for relaxation and lovely for drying the flowers for herb sachets or for dried flower arrangements.

Lemon verbena and scented-leaved pelargoniums are not hardy, so you will need to bring them indoors for the winter. If you don't have room for the old plants, root cuttings in small pots in late summer and keep these on a windowsill indoors for the winter instead.

ANNUAL HERBS

BASIL, CHERVIL, DILL, PARSLEY AND CORIANDER Grow them in moist, fertile soil, where they get sun for at least half the day. Some annual herbs, such as basil and coriander, quickly run to seed, so with these you need to sow several crops each year. The seeds of coriander are good for Indian cooking, but there's nothing better than fresh coriander leaves on your curry. The curled form of parsley is the most popular for garnishes. In mild winters we've had fresh parsley still available at Christmas time.

HOW TO GROW HERBS IN CONTAINERS
Use a large container — a terracotta or glazed ceramic pot looks good planted with herbs. You can buy special herb planters, although they can be a lot more fuss and hard work than ordinary pots, which look just as good. Place a layer of bits of broken clay pot or a handful of coarse gravel or pebbles in the bottom for drainage, and half-fill the container with soil-based potting mixture. Stand the plants inside, still in their pots, while you decide how you want to arrange them. Then take the herbs out of their pots, stand the rootballs in place and fill the gaps with more mixture. Water well. Soil-based potting mixture contains enough nutrients, so you won't need to give any extra feed for three months. After that, the easiest way to feed is to push a slow-release feed pellet or stick into the middle of the pot. Then, each time you water, a steady supply of plant food is automatically released. If you do go to the trouble or expense of a special herb planter, or are given one as a gift, always bear in mind the ultimate size and spread of the herbs. Put small herbs like thyme or parsley in the planting pockets and don't put anything large in the top, as it will be hard to remove after a couple of years. Choose something like chives, which have shallow roots.

Herbs can be a good choice for window boxes, but try to choose compact types like marjoram or chamomile. Shrubby plants like sage or rosemary will need replacing often.

GROWING EVERGREEN HERBS FROM CUTTINGS

- Cut about 7.5 cm (3 in)-long shoots from the tips of young stems any time during the summer, strip off the leaves from the bottom half of the stem and push several cuttings into a pot of soil-based seed mix, about 2.5 cm (1 in) apart.
- Water and cover the pot with a loose plastic bag, but only water after this if the soil is drying out. If they are too damp, they will rot.
- Stand it on a windowsill indoors out of the sun, and most cuttings will have rooted in about eight weeks. (Bay takes a lot longer.)
- When they are rooted, pot each cutting in a separate pot and pinch out the growing tips to encourage them to grow bushy. Use this method for evergreen herbs such as rosemary, plus lavender, lemon verbena and scented-leaved pelargoniums.

GROWING ANNUAL HERBS FROM SEED

Sow seeds thinly in pots on a warm windowsill or in a greenhouse in spring. They should germinate rapidly this way, although I have known parsley to take its time. Instead of pricking out each seedling individually, wait until they are 2.5 cm (1 in) high and then tip them out, divide them up into three to five clumps and pot complete clumps. This gives you much bushier plants straightaway. When they are big enough, harden them off and plant the herbs in containers or out in the garden. Keep the spares in pots on the kitchen windowsill to use in cooking while you are waiting for the rest to grow. Don't put frost-tender herbs, such as basil, outside until a week or more after the last frost.

DIVIDING PERENNIAL HERBS

You can propagate herbs that die down in winter, such as mint and chives, by digging up clumps in spring and dividing them like perennial flowers. You can usually pull herbs apart with your fingers. Replant the pieces in the garden or in pots. Divide chives by tearing the ball of roots in two. First shake off as much soil as you can so you can see what you are doing.

Chapter 20

Growing Roses

THEY DO GROW ON YOU!

Until we moved to our current garden 13 years ago, I didn't have much time for roses. Those we inherited were always looked after, but new plants were rarely added to our gardens. I think I'd been put off by rose beds of prickly, bare branches dominating whole borders and being told that roses liked to be kept to themselves. When I saw the other possibilities roses had to offer, with mixed hedges covered in wild dog roses in early summer, and finally had room for large pergolas and walls for ramblers to really get going on, I changed my mind.

Roses are the most popular garden plants ever, found in nearly 90 per cent of gardens. There are several different groups, each with their own flowering seasons and size that make them best for particular situations. Formal rose beds are not necessary and modern compact kinds can be used like any flowering shrub, and even planted in containers. So, there are enough reasons for growing roses in any garden to warrant their own chapter. There are about 250 distinct species and all are hardy and deciduous.

ROSE TERMS
NAMED VARIETY is the cultivated rose with large, spectacular flowers.
THE ROOTSTOCK is a form of wild rose specially grown for this purpose. The flowers look wild and rootstocks often have rosehips.
SUCKERS are strong shoots growing directly from roots of the rootstock. They often grow more vigorously if the plant has been dug up and moved, or when the roots have been damaged with a hoe when weeding.

ANATOMY OF A ROSE
Roses are actually two plants joined together, with the stems of one variety growing on the roots of another. For the gardener, grafted plants can create work, as the rootstock often sends up strong suckers that grow faster than the named variety and unless dealt with, they can take over the plant. The stems of rootstocks are relatively thorn-free and their leaves usually have a different number of leaflets. Trace back a suspect stem. If it originates underground, it is almost certainly a

sucker. Dig carefully round it with a trowel and find the point where it emerges from a root, then tear it out. If you cut suckers off at ground level, they grow back worse than ever. If you find it easier, you can spray suckers carefully with a weedkiller in spring when they are soft and first push through the soil, but protect surrounding plants. This is a desperate measure to take.

THE DIFFERENT TYPES OF ROSES

It's always a good idea to try to find out what sort of roses you're dealing with, as pruning needs vary and if you're not careful you could miss out on a lot of flowers, like I have done in the past!

- MODERN BUSH roses include the popular hybrid teas and floribundas that flower almost continuously from early summer to the first autumn frosts. Prune them hard each year in early spring, apply a rose food and mulch generously with well-watered organic matter. These roses used to be grown in formal rose beds on their own, but nowadays they are often planted in mixed borders.
- STANDARD ROSES are just bush roses grafted on to a tall stem to make them look like small flowering trees. Don't prune standard roses hard, or you may find that all you have left is the stem of the rootstock. Just prune lightly in mid-spring to reshape the head of the plant.
- PATIO ROSES are very compact, free-flowering versions of bush roses and ideal for growing in tubs. Prune lightly in early spring to keep them in shape. Feed and mulch as described above for bush roses.
- GROUND-COVER ROSES are low-growing, spreading or semi-creeping kinds, good for covering sunny banks or the fronts of borders if they are free of perennial weeds. It's hard work weeding through a carpet of prickly stems, without ripping your hands to pieces. Prune lightly to keep them in shape in early spring. When prostrate ground-cover roses such as 'Nozomi' are grafted on to stems, they make delightful, small, weeping trees — superb plants for all-year-round containers or as the centrepiece of a small flower bed.
- MINIATURE ROSES are much more fragile. Although often sold in pots as houseplants, they are best grown outdoors in a sheltered, sunny spot, in rich but well-drained ground. They do well in raised beds and

containers. No pruning is needed, but use scissors to remove dead shoots in late spring.

- SHRUB ROSES are more closely related to the wild species, with simple flowers, often followed by large or colourful rosehips. They are ideal for more natural gardens and can make good prickly hedging, but they can also be grown in mixed borders. Regular pruning isn't needed; just tidy the shape in early spring if they need it.

- OLD-FASHIONED ROSES are hybrids with long-lost pedigrees, often dating back a century or more. They have characteristic blowsy flowers or shallow, bowl-shaped heads divided into 'quarters', quite unlike modern roses. Some have exceptional perfume. Treat old-fashioned roses as if they were flowering shrubs and grow them in mixed borders or in cottage-style gardens, underplanted with a mixture of low, spreading perennials and spring bulbs. These provide colour and interest outside the rose's short flowering season, which only lasts for a few weeks in summer. Prune after flowering, removing the dead flowers, plus 15 cm (6 in) of stem. Thin out a few old overcrowded branches in winter.

- CLIMBING ROSES look very much like ordinary bush roses, except that instead of being bushy, they have a permanent framework of thick stems tied up to a wall or structure. Very little pruning is normally needed; just remove dead flower heads with a good length of stem in summer.

- RAMBLER ROSES have quite a different type of growth, more like blackberry 'canes'. Vigorous varieties need pruning quite hard in autumn. Cut back the stems that have flowered to the point where they join a strong, new, unflowered shoot. Non-vigorous varieties only need deadheading. Keep your ramblers under control, or you will find you need a neck like a giraffe to see the flowers properly!

Climbing and rambler roses are ideal for covering arches, pergolas or trellis with summer colour. Some varieties flower once, some twice-yearly, and some for much of the summer, so check when you buy.

PRUNING RAMBLERS AND CLIMBERS

- *RAMBLERS* In late summer, after flowering has finished, cut out any very old or diseased shoots right back to the base. Don't cut back the younger, healthy shoots.

Go along the remaining main branches and prune back all the side shoots to between two and four pairs of leaves from the main stem.

• *CLIMBERS* Climbers sometimes need careful pruning to restrict their height and spread and to keep them flowering well towards the base. In late summer or autumn cut out dead, diseased or damaged shoots. If there are many old stems, cut one or two back to the base of the plant. On old climbers cut one or two thick shoots to about 30 cm (12 in) to encourage new shoots to grow from the base. Work along each of the remaining main stems and reduce the length of all the sideshoots to about 15 cm (6 in).

DEADHEADING

All roses need deadheading regularly. Cut off the dead head with 5–10 cm (2–4 in) of stem, below the lowest bloom in the bunch. Cut just above a leaf and a new flowering shoot will soon grow.

Apply more rose food and water well in.

CHOOSING ROSES

With so many varieties around and so many colours, shapes and perfumes, the best way to discover what you like is to go and see the roses growing. That way you get a better idea than from glossy catalogues with enhanced colour printing and won't end up with a load of roses that look the same red, orange or pink, but don't quite fit in. You can't tell a perfume from a catalogue either. Give me white, scented roses anytime.

• '*BALLERINA*' is a modern shrub rose that flowers all summer.

• '*SWEET DREAMS*' is a patio rose needing a rich potting mixture and regular feeding.

• *ROSA MUNDI* dates back to the fourteenth century but is still popular for its stripy flowers. It is a small, bushy plant with a short flowering season in early summer.

• *ROSA RUGOSA* is a suitable hedging rose for windy areas.

• *ROSA SPINOSISSIMA ALTAICA* has large pale yellow single roses.

• '*MADAME ALFRED CARRIERE*' grows to 6 m (20 ft), so needs care and plenty of room. The flowers are double white with a pinkish tinge and have a wonderful perfume. Ideal for planting near an opening window or patio door.

Chapter 21

Growing Vegetables and Soft Fruit

Fruit and vegetables are particularly rewarding to grow and with concerns increasing over food production using chemicals, many people are reverting to growing a few organic vegetables of their own. You don't have to have a huge garden or allotment to grow salad crops and you can even grow some new potatoes in containers or plastic bags to use up all that mint that's taken over the herb border!

You can enjoy the results of your labours on your dinner plate, and many gardeners find great satisfaction from nurturing seedlings which grow into fantastic-flavoured, fresh produce that you can dig up, or pick, and eat. You can feel quite benevolent (or smug) with a heavy crop of beans that you just have to give away, because there are so many of them that you can't even freeze any more.

Before you get carried away, however, bear in mind that there is, initially, the small matter of preparing the ground, looking after the plants through late frosts, drought, flood and pestilence. Still, you can start small, with a couple of growbags, and work up.

The difference between a mediocre and bumper crop can usually be accounted for by the amount of care and attention the plants receive. Many of the tips and techniques suggested in the following pages will help you to achieve better or bigger crops. An early start can produce crops weeks ahead of the normal time, which means tasty home-grown produce earlier and at a time when it is more expensive in the shops.

CHOOSING A SITE

THERE'S A PLACE . . .
Make your kitchen garden as attractive and productive as possible through careful planning. If space is limited, try growing some of the more decorative vegetables and herbs in flower beds.

Almost all vegetables and most fruits require a sunny position to do well. Place fruit trees where they will not cast shade over the vegetables.

The conventional method of growing vegetables is in long rows. This is a convenient way to grow them, and if the rows are kept well weeded, a vegetable garden can look very attractive, but if you have the space it's far better to divide the plot into smaller beds.

A 1.2 m (4 ft) bed system is popular with organic gardeners and those who want to minimise digging. Beds of this width are wide enough for cultivation to be carried out easily from the paths on each side. This means that you don't have to walk on the soil and compact it, so the earth is kept in better condition. You also concentrate the feeding on the planting areas, rather than on generally covering the area where you'll be walking as well, so save precious compost. If the ground has been well prepared first and is regularly mulched with organic material, you should not have to dig. You may need to adjust the normal spacings for the plants, as there is no need to leave room to walk between the rows.

A surprisingly large range of vegetables can be grown in containers — even crops like peas, beans and potatoes. Some vegetables, such as red lettuces, beetroot and rhubarb chard, are decorative enough to be grown among flowers, if you don't mind leaving gaps once you begin to harvest them.

CROP ROTATION
By rotating the places where you plant various crops, you can reduce the risk of certain pests and diseases building up in the soil and you can group together plants that need similar soil fertility. Some crops dislike newly manured ground and some crops help to improve nitrogen levels in the soil.

Some gardeners use a four-year rotation, but three years is good enough for most of us. Keep one part of the plot for perennial crops, such as asparagus or rhubarb, or Jerusalem artichokes which can be left in place. Divide the rest into three areas:
• *GROUP A* Choose from beetroot, carrots, celeriac, courgettes, garlic, leeks, onions, shallots, potatoes, peppers, pumpkins or tomatoes. Potatoes and root crops are particularly good for clearing the soil of perennial

weeds and for improving soil condition. These crops benefit from good digging and the addition of manure. You can feed crops during the growing season as well.

• *GROUP B* All types of beans, peas, spinach and lettuce. Beans and peas help fix nitrogen in the soil, so as well as providing a good crop of healthy veg, you'll improve the soil for future years. Digging and a general fertiliser at the beginning of the season are best.

• *GROUP C* Cabbage, broccoli, sprouts, cauliflower, swede, kale, kohl rabi, radishes. These plants may need lime to bring the soil to a pH of 6.5−7.0. (See page 15 if you missed this section.) General fertilizer in spring is best, with additional feeding if necessary, as the season progresses. It's a lot easier to stick to vegetables that grow happily. If you don't like these vegetables, you can always rest the soil, or grow flowers for the season.

Over the course of three years, you can then give your vegetables what they want, as well as giving the soil a chance to improve.

Plant from the groups as follows:

Year One	Group A	Group B	Group C
Year Two	Group B	Group C	Group A
Year Three	Group C	Group A	Group B

SOWING INTERCROPS
To make the most of space available, grow quickly maturing crops between slower-growing ones, e.g. lettuce between sweetcorn.

If you lift early potatoes you can still grow lettuce or radishes in the same bed.

If you mix radish seed with parsnip seed, you can harvest the fast-growing radishes before the parsnips notice they need the space.

GROUNDWORK AND PLANTING

A vegetable plot normally needs digging over at least once a year, unless you've really cracked the mulching, no dig method. There are bound to be some new perennial weeds that have escaped your best intentions and/or notice. If you didn't read the section on digging (page 14), do so now. Before planting seeds or vegetable seedlings, rake over and remove any weeds, especially perennials.

Follow the directions on the packet, and save the packet, even when empty, as you'll be surprised how quickly you forget the information about care, crops, etc. Unfinished packs of seed should be stored in a cool, dry place so that they can be used at a later date.

RAISED BEDS

Raised beds can be used for a wide variety of vegetables. The deep soil means you can plant them closer together than usual — about half to two-thirds normal spacing. This means less work for you, as the plants smother out weeds, and you get more crops from the space. You can grow any vegetables this way.

KNOW THE DRILL

Using a garden line to keep long rows straight not only makes the garden look tidier, it also helps to identify seedlings as they emerge. This doesn't need to be fancy; a long line of string, tied to a strong stick each end will do the trick. Put one stick in the soil and pull the line taut, winding any surplus string onto the other stick. Put the other stick in the ground at the end of the planting row. Shorter lines can be kept straight by using a bamboo cane. Use a hoe or rake to make the drill. Follow the instructions for depth on the packet of seeds. Water the soil first, then sprinkle seeds as thinly and as evenly as possible. This stops the seeds being washed away by watering afterwards. Cover the seeds by shuffling your feet along the sides of the drill, or rake the soil back over gently, in the direction of the drill and not across it.

MULTIPLE ROWS OF PEAS AND FRENCH BEANS

Some seeds, like peas and French beans, are sown in multiple rows or zigzags. Make a wide drill with a hoe and space the seeds in the bottom. These larger seeds are easier to place accurately by hand. Pull the soil back over and water in. I always put old cloche frames over the rows and cover with netting straightaway. This stops birds pecking at the green shoots and reminds me exactly where I've planted, as sticks get removed easily and mysteriously.

PLANTING POTATOES

Growing potatoes is easy once the digging's been done properly, and being able to dig your own new spuds, cook them and eat them within the hour is a truly rewarding experience. Chit the tuber first, then plant them 9–13 cm (4–5 in) deep, 30 cm (12 in) apart. Leave 60 cm (24 in) between rows. Apart from earthing up as the plants start to grow, there is little else to do until harvesting your delicious crop. This involves drawing up the soil into sloping ridges on each side of each row. This will prevent the developing tubers from going green and being inedible when exposed to the light.

MAKING AN EARLY START WITH CLOCHES

If you're really keen to get started early, or your gardening is dictated by the time you have available, rather than the weather conditions, early in the season, then using cloches may be the answer. They are the next best thing to a greenhouse or a cold frame and have the advantage of protecting plants in the ground where you want them to produce. Put the cloches over the ground for a couple of weeks to warm up the soil before you plant.

TENTS

There are all sorts of cloches available, but the simplest and cheapest are plastic tent varieties which are rigid and self-supporting. Avoid glass varieties if you have children or dogs who want to play ball. Pay attention to the ends, otherwise you risk turning the cloche into a wind tunnel or a cosy place for the local cats to sleep.

TUNNELS

Plastic tunnel cloches are also quite cheap, but make sure the plastic is held firmly by securely fitted wire hoops. Otherwise, like our first (polythene) greenhouse in Yorkshire, you might end up with materials for a kite instead and watch it sail away over the fence into the sunset at the first sign of wind. Plastic can be pulled taut and secured both ends, but the wind can do a lot of damage, and make a dreadful noise if the plastic is allowed to flap about. The wire supports can later be used to support netting which will keep birds off.

FLOATING CLOCHES

These can be used in autumn as well as spring, to protect vegetables until they mature. Perforated plastic film will protect seedlings and is cheap, but won't last very long. Some netting gives protection from light frosts and pests and can be peeled back to weed as the seedlings grow. Horticultural fleece will protect crops from a few degrees of frost and will deter pests, too. Once the seedlings have been sown, pull the fleece over the area, holding it down with large stones, bricks or earth.

SOWING SEEDS FOR EARLY HARVESTS

Many vegetables can be started off in pots and seed trays so that they are already growing well when you plant them out. This is also a good method for brassicas (members of the cabbage family). The plants will have a start which may make them more resistant to disease like club-root.

POTS AND MODULES

Use a good sterilised compost and clean pots or modules. Modules are good for lettuce which are planted out while still small and don't need so much compost or space. Put three seeds into each pot and if more than one germinates, thin to leave just the strongest. They are also ideal for leeks, onions, carrots and beetroot, although you can leave the seeds without thinning. You won't get prize exhibits, but you will get hassle free growing, which you can thin by harvesting as the vegetables grow.

After hardening off (see chapter 12), water the seedlings, knock them out of their pots and plant in the garden. Make sure you keep the rootball intact. I always start some of my runner beans in pots so that we get early crops and so that the tender young plants are not so attractive to slugs and birds. Then I top up with other beans, sown straight into the ground about three weeks later.

GUTTERING

This method means there is even less root disturbance when planting out. Sow seeds in a length of plastic guttering filled with compost. Cover them with soil and keep in a greenhouse until the seedlings are about 8 cm (3 in) tall. Thin as necessary. When you are ready to transfer them to the ground make a wide drill with a hoe and slide the compost in one long sausage into the ground. Water well and firm the plants in. This is very successful with peas and other vegetables as well as with flowers.

CHITTING FOR EARLY POTATOES

If you chit the tubers of potatoes you will have a crop earlier than expected. Place the potatoes in trays and keep them in a light, frost-free place until they start to shoot. When the shoots are about 2 cm ($^3/_4$ in) rub all but two or three shoots off the tubers before planting them out. Alternatively, try growing them in a bin liner.

SUPPORTING AND STAKING BEANS

Runner beans, climbing French beans and tall peas need some form of support. We always put the support for beans in place when we plant them. Peas support themselves by curling their tendrils around sticks. As the seeds start to grow, I remove the netting, before the peas use it as a climbing frame, and replace with twiggy sticks from prunings. We use the tops of bamboo as well, which are very good for keeping the birds off as they rustle in the breeze. The larger portions of bamboo are used for runner beans to climb up, as described below.

Nylon netting can be used to support both beans and peas. Stretch 10 cm (4 in) mesh between two stout posts and tie on securely. This method does offer quite a lot of wind resistance when the plants are fully grown and heavy with beans. You may have to help the young beans by threading through to start them climbing.

BAMBOOZLED
We use bamboo canes for several reasons, the main one being that we have a monster clump of bamboo which we inherited with the garden. One way of keeping it in check is to crop it each spring. We supply the neighbours, too! Bamboo canes have several handy features, as well as being very cheap to buy. They are not too unsightly while the plants are growing (especially ours, which are striped while still fresh), they are flexible, light and extremely versatile. Because you need to rotate your crops, bamboo canes are easily removed for storage, or disposed of and replaced for the next season.

TWO TENTS?
If you have just a few runners, grow them in a wigwam of about five canes, tied securely at the top. Push the canes at least 30 cm (12 in) into the soil. You can grow them at the back of a flower border, or in a large tub as follows. Start the beans off by winding them round a cane to keep them off the ground, away from the dreaded slugs. Be prepared to rewind them, if you've wound them the wrong way, as they will grow out, away towards another post. Follow the lead of those already winding their way upwards.

For a whole row, insert two rows of 2.4 m (8 ft) canes opposite each other at a slight angle, 30 cm (12 in) apart. Slide a horizontal cane along the top, in the V formed by crossing the canes over. Pull downwards to secure firmly in place and tie each intersection to provide extra strength. This forms a ridge like the top of a tent and lots of strong triangle shapes. By the time these beans are covered, the winds may be quite strong, and the last thing you want is a collapsed frame. If one cane isn't long enough for the top, just overlap another one in the groove and tie in place.

GROWING ONIONS FROM SETS

Make shallow drills with a hoe, about 30 cm (12 in) apart. Space the onion sets about 15 cm (6 in) apart and press firmly into the soil so that just the tips protrude above the soil when the drill is filled in. Birds might cause a problem by tugging on the stems while the roots are getting established, but by gently replanting, or protecting with cloches or netting, they should recover quickly.

MAKING THE MOST OF A SMALL SALAD BED
- Straight rows make the most of every bit of space, so use a cane laid across the top of the bed as a guide when sowing.
- Make your bed the same width as 'bought' cloches or rolls of horticultural fleece. Use these to cover crops for protection from the weather, so that you can make earlier spring sowings and keep late crops going longer than usual.
- Space rows of crops closer together. As the soil is deeper than in a normally prepared vegetable garden, the roots go down further.
- Sow alternate fast- and slow-growing crops, or upright and spreading crops (such as spring onions and lettuce). That way, you can reduce the spacing.
- As soon as one row of lettuces is almost ready for cutting, sow some more seeds.
- Sow little and often to avoid having masses of lettuces all ready at the same time. A pinch of seed every two weeks should be enough; it saves waste and also means you don't spend so much on seed.

GROWING SALAD CROPS

You don't need much room to grow salad leaves; they are so productive that a bed measuring 90 x 180 cm (3 x 6 ft) is enough to keep a family of salad-lovers going all summer. They are very little work, too. In a bed with raised sides, the soil is deeper than usual, which means that you can plant crops close together, but don't need to tread on the ground after it has been prepared.

Before sowing, sprinkle blood, fish and bone fertiliser over the soil at the rate recommended and rake well in. To keep crops growing vigorously, apply diluted organic liquid feeds or liquid seaweed extract when they are roughly half-grown. Keep the soil in a salad bed moist at all times, as salad crops are very shallow-rooted. If the soil dries out badly, leaf salads often bolt and lettuces may taste bitter.

Hoe carefully between rows until the plant leaves touch and cover the ground. Hoe very shallowly to avoid damaging roots. As soon as a row of salad has been cut, clear up the leaves, weeds and debris, then lightly fork over the ground, rake it level and sow or plant the next crop straightaway.

POPULAR SALAD CROPS

• *LETTUCE* Sow summer varieties from mid-spring to midsummer. Sow fast-maturing varieties in late summer to cover with cloches for autumn use. Grow a few of each of several different types of lettuce for a constant supply of varied, colourful and interesting salads.

• *CABBAGE LETTUCE* Traditional round green lettuce. Small varieties, such as 'Tom Thumb', are ideal for compact salad beds as you plant them closer together and so fit more into the space.

• *COS LETTUCE (ROMAINE)* Superb flavour, but tall varieties need tying round with raffia when half-grown to make them form hearts. They often bolt in hot or dry weather. Semi-cos varieties, such as 'Little Gem', are easy to grow, don't need tying up and taste delicious.

• *OAK LEAF LETTUCE* Good flavour and pretty leaf shapes make them suitable for mixed leaf salads or as garnishes. You can usually pick a few leaves and leave the rest to grow.

• *CUT-AND-COME-AGAIN LETTUCE* Varieties allow you to cut a few leaves at a time without harvesting the entire plant. You can do this for several months before the plant runs to seed.

• *ROCKET* Sow two to three times per year, from early spring to midsummer. Both the flowers and the leaves are edible.

• *SPRING ONIONS* Sow onions thickly in spring and thin out the plants gradually. Use the plant you remove as spring onions at any stage, from baby to full-grown. This way, one row will last you all season.

• *ORIENTAL LEAVES* Sow a mixture of Chinese cabbage, pak choi, mizuna, etc., in early summer and cut as baby leaves. Or use thinnings in salads, leaving the remaining plants spaced 15—20 cm (6—8 in) apart to form hearts to use in autumn.

• *BABY SPINACH LEAVES* Sow little and often from early spring under cloches to late spring, then again in late summer for an autumn crop. In summer, spinach runs to seed too quickly to make it worth growing.

• *HERBS* Grow a single row containing a few plants each of leaf coriander (cilantro), flat-leaved parsley, chives and other good leafy herbs for salad use.

TOMATOES

Raising something you can eat is one of the most satisfying of gardening experiences, and tomatoes are among the most rewarding crops. If you can't be bothered with growing lettuce, at least give tomatoes a try. You can pick a few every day throughout late summer and early autumn. Home-grown tomatoes, ripened fully on the vine, taste far better than those that you buy. You don't need a greenhouse if you grow outdoor varieties; choose a warm sheltered spot. The plants look good enough to grow on the patio. Grow them in large tubs 30—38 cm (12—15 in) in diameter and stand them in front of a sunny wall, where they'll enjoy the reflected heat and light. This also makes the plants easy to support, as you can tie them up to a trellis or panel. You can buy plants from a garden centre, ready to pot on, but they are quite easy to grow from seed on a kitchen windowsill, if you haven't got a greenhouse. Start early in this case, as the growing season isn't that long, especially if you live in a cold area. You will need to repot the seedlings two or three times before they are ready to go outside, so be prepared for the need for space indoors to avoid frost damage. The plants also need a lot of light to prevent them getting 'leggy'. If you only want a couple of plants, persuade someone with a greenhouse to start them off for you.

GROWING TOMATOES IN TUBS

• *ORDINARY CORDON VARIETIES* Fill a tub with potting mixture and plant the tomato seedling quite deeply, so that the pair of long, narrow, seed leaves at the base of the plant (which don't look like normal tomato leaves) are flush with the surface of the compost. Unless the pot is standing at the foot of a trellis, push a 1.5 m (5 ft) cane alongside the plant so that you can tie in the stem for support. Use soft string and tie it in a loose figure of eight so that the plant is not pulled in tightly towards the cane.

Water lightly, just enough to settle the potting mixture around the plant's roots, and water sparingly until the first fruit starts to swell. Each week, tie the new growth up to the stake and nip out the sideshoots which grow in the V shaped space between the main stem and the main side branches regularly. When six or so sprays of fruit have set, remove the growing tip two leaves above the top spray of flowers. The fruits can get quite heavy as they swell and late tomatoes are unlikely to ripen.

• *BUSH VARIETIES* These don't need such a lot of support and you don't pinch out the side shoots. You still need to limit the number of sprays, especially if grown in tubs. I used a variety of yellow cherry tomatoes one year for growing in hanging baskets. Very decorative, and handy to pick while passing!

• *BEEFSTEAK TOMATOES* When sliced, the large, often rather misshapen, fruits are like tomato steaks and are ideal for sandwiches, tomato salads or grilling. However, being so big, the fruits are often slow to ripen. At the end of the summer, when it starts getting cold at night, tomatoes ripen more slowly, so pick off all the remaining fruit and take it indoors. Small green tomatoes will never ripen, so use for chutney. Full-sized tomatoes will ripen if you put them in a drawer, or a large loose bag with a ripe tomato, apple or banana. Keep cool, and the tomatoes will ripen in about 7–10 days.

SOFT FRUIT

Fruit growing can be very rewarding, and you don't need a huge garden or an orchard, either Chapter 16 dealt with fruit trees and some of the ways of growing them in a small garden. Almost all fruits prefer a sunny position, but they can be trained to fit in with other planting. Some fruits can be grown in tubs and even rampant blackberries can be trained on wires so that they don't take over. You could even train them over an arch, but watch out for the thorns as a hazard for children and visitors.

• *STRAWBERRIES* are very easy to grow. Buy certified, disease-free plants and prepare the soil well with plenty of garden compost. Most strawberry plants are sold in pots, so all you need to do is water them well before planting and plant at their original depth. Plant in autumn or spring for preference. If you can bear to, remove any flowers the first year so that the plants become well established before carrying a crop. Strawberries can also be grown in pots or special strawberry planters. Water well and don't let them dry out. Strawberries reproduce on runners, with a mini plant growing from each runner. To increase your stock of plants, or to replace old, tired plants, allow a few of the strongest plants to develop a runner each. Nip out the rest, as they will weaken the plant. Don't sever the baby plants from the parent, but peg them into the soil, where, in a few weeks, the new plant will have established roots. You can then transplant the new strawberry. I often pot a few of the extras and then put them in the greenhouse for an early crop the following year.

As the strawberries ripen, cover with a net. Our net is squirrel-proof, having lost the entire green crop a few years ago to a pair of local tree rats. You may also need to protect the soil around the plants with matting or straw to protect the fruit. Watch out for slugs and snails too.

• *CURRANTS AND GOOSEBERRIES* Blackcurrants, white and redcurrants are easy to grow, although you need quite a few bushes to provide a decent crop. They need to be spaced 1.2–1.5 m (4–5 ft) apart and require regular pruning to maintain crops. Blackcurrants are pruned in a different way from the white and red types, as are gooseberries, so be careful.

• *RASPBERRIES, BLACKBERRIES, LOGANBERRIES AND TAYBERRIES* Raspberries can be grown against a fence to save space. Plant raspberries about 45 cm (1^1/$_2$ ft) apart in shallow, composted trench. Cut the cane back to about 25 cm (10 in). In midsummer cut the original stem back to ground level and tie in the new canes to supporting wires. To make harvesting easy, train the stems to wires stretched between two posts. Space the wires about 30 cm (12 in) apart. After fruiting, cut back the canes that have fruited, leaving the rest for next season's crop to grow on. If they grow taller than their support, bend them over and tie in place again.

Blackberries and hybrids need a bit more room, so space 2.4–5 m (8–15 ft) apart, depending on the variety.

Chapter 22

First Aid for Plants

FRIEND OR FOE? THE GREEN APPROACH

Even the best kept gardens will have problems. It's not only the weather you have to deal with. Running a successful garden means keeping on top of small problems, before they grow into larger ones. You can get a lot of help from beneficial insects, birds, frogs, toads, hedgehogs and worms, as long as you don't kill them off with chemicals. Controlling pests the natural way is better for us all and you have a lot more fun watching them at work. If you spray the aphids, you will poison the beneficial insects as well. If you don't have insects, you will miss out on a lot of interesting birds and you won't be helping with pollination.

You can buy beneficial insect predators and parasites to tackle a wide range of indoor and outdoor pests. Biological controls for greenfly and whitefly are most effective if used in a greenhouse. Living organisms cannot be stored, so you buy them by mail order or via a garden centre. When delivered, use them straightaway. Better still, grow your own!

BENEFICIAL INSECTS
These include:

- Ladybirds
- Hoverflies
- Spiders
- Earwigs
- Beetles
- Lacewings

See Appendix 1, page 150 for details

PLANTS THAT ATTRACT BENEFICIAL INSECTS
Yellow flowers seem to attract more insects than some other colours.

Choose some old-fashioned hardy annuals:

- Pot or French marigolds
- Californian poppy
- Poached egg flower
- Verbascum
- Wildflower mixes

PLANTS TO ATTRACT BUTTERFLIES

Butterflies like warmth and nectar-rich blue flowers.
If you are willing to leave a small patch of nettles that
you can use for liquid feed, you will also encourage red
admirals, peacocks, small tortoiseshells and commas to
lay their eggs as well.

- Ceanothus
- Buddleia
- Berberis
- Clematis
- Michaelmas daisies
- Lesser periwinkle
- Globe thistle
- Evening primrose
- Thyme
- Rosemary
- Lavender

WILD AREAS

Try to look upon weeds as wildflowers and a source of
food for wildlife. Lots of wildflowers look really good in a
mixed border. Our garden is full of foxgloves in late
spring, entirely self-set, and providing lots of nectar. If
you can spare a small area of lawn that you don't mow,
weed or feed, you will encourage a lot more insects,
benefit from less mowing and establish a variety of
wildflowers. Don't dig up wildflowers from the
countryside or hedgerows. For a quick start, get a
neighbour to give you a clod of turf from their wild
patch. If not, you can buy packets of wild seeds.

BIRD HELPERS

As well as bringing life and song to the garden, birds
manage to consume a huge number of pests. See
Appendix 1, page 150.

NEST BOXES

If you haven't got trees or large shrubs for birds to nest
in, you can encourage them by providing nest boxes.
These need to be put in place in winter so that birds can
get used to them before the breeding season. Insect nest
boxes, bat boxes, and even hedgehog boxes are also
available to encourage extra help.

ANIMAL HELPERS

Hedgehogs, frogs, toads and shrews are among the
beneficial visitors to your garden, providing a great
service in dealing with slugs and snails. By letting them

get down to a spot of free dining, you are helping the environment become a balanced ecosystem, where artificial additives are unnecessary and natural forces come into play. If you kill the slugs, you either kill their natural predators, or drive them away to somewhere they are appreciated. Food chains are a fact of life. See Appendix 1, page 152 for some common pest problems and solutions.

DETERRING UNWELCOME VISITORS

However much of a nature lover you are, the sight of your hard work disappearing because of uninvited 'pests' will test your principles. Other people's pets, as well as squirrels, birds, rabbits, foxes and even deer can wreak havoc.

BIRDS

Keep them off your newly planted crops and strawberries with netting. Make sure the edges are secure so that birds don't get caught in the netting and hurt themselves. Use strips of foil or unwanted free CD or computer discs, strung up to catch the light and deter them.

Give smaller birds a chance to thrive by planting dense, prickly shrubs, where they can hide from magpies, sparrowhawks and cats.

Watch out for your pond, if you have herons in the area. They can shovel up a load of frogspawn faster than you can shout at them, and they also love fishing in shallow water. Seagulls are also a problem where fish are concerned and I shall always remember as a child, watching our prize goldfish flying away in the beak of a herring gull. Mesh or netting will stop this, but doesn't look very nice.

CATS

Even as a cat lover, there are times when I hate them. Apart from their natural tendencies as predators, which is upsetting enough, when dear old Sid catches a mouse (Well done, Sid), or a young bird (You evil cat, get away!), there's the problem of your newly dug patch turning into a giant litter tray. Our worst decision was to gravel a long walkway under a pergola. The local moggies thought we had opened a public convenience! If the cats are used to including your garden as their territory, it can take some time to get rid of them. Here are some suggestions:

- Site nesting boxes and bird tables well away from places a cat can get to.
- Scatter prickly prunings like holly, roses and berberis where cats like to walk or squat.
- Placing citrus fruits cut in half or pepper can deter some cats.
- Chemical deterrents in powder, liquid or gel form seem to work for a while.
- Get a cat of your own — or a dog!

SQUIRRELS

Although a lot of people think squirrels are lovely, they are really only tree rodents. They are quite vicious creatures and can damage young trees and shrubs and eat vast quantities of fruit and nuts before you've had a chance to try any yourself. They also attack birds' nests, eating eggs and fledglings, and can cause a lot of damage to tap roots, leaves and buds. I don't know how to get rid of them, but we've managed to get them to nest elsewhere and we certainly don't encourage their acrobatic skills by feeding them. If you feed birds, site tables away from trees and rooftops to discourage squirrels taking a leap. They'll find a way eventually, whatever you try. The cat gives our resident rodents a good run for their money, however.

WEEDS AND PREVENTION

Weeds are basically any plants growing in the wrong place. Fast-growing native plants that spread quickly from seed, such as groundsel, or by rampant underground runners, like bindweed, are the commonest sorts. Some cultivated plants, however, can become a problem when they establish themselves too well. For the first few years after you dig up an uncultivated plot, you'll get couch grass and tough perennial weeds reappearing unless you take drastic action. Seeds can stay in the ground, waiting for their chance to germinate for years and years: they don't all grow at the same time, but come up a few at a time. That's why weeds are so successful.

The best way to deal with perennial weeds, other than prevention, is to dig them out with the root intact and throw them away, or burn them. Perennial weeds have roots which stay in the soil during the winter and come up again every year unless you get them out. Even if you chop off the tops, they just grow again. Perennials include:

- Bindweed
- Buttercups
- Couch grass
- Dock
- Ground elder
- Horsetail
- Nettles
- Thistles

Digging without chopping roots is therefore the key, but easier said than done, with bindweed and couch grass in particular. Hoeing or using a rotovator just encourages all the little bits of root to grow even better.

Annual weeds include:

- Fat hen
- Groundsel
- Knotgrass
- Mayweed
- Poppy
- Shepherd's purse

These are more easily dealt with before seeding, although you need to keep an eye open for two or three 'harvests' a year.

See Appendix 1, page 153, for getting to grips with weeds.

WEED PREVENTION

MULCHING
Mulching is a much quicker option than regular hand weeding or hoeing. Annual mulching involves spreading a thick layer of organic material between plants each spring. For long-lasting results, especially on small areas, for instance a small front garden, or area round a water feature, cover the soil in a weed-proof membrane. You can plant through this and, hopefully, virtually eliminate weeding for good.
- *LOOSE MULCHES* A mulch round plants in spring smothers germinating seeds and helps to seal in moisture,

so that plants don't dry out so quickly in summer. It also provides insulation to roots, preventing overheating in summer and frost damage in winter. Worms pull the material down into the soil, helping to steadily improve it. In early spring the soil should be moist, well weeded and loosened with a fork. Spread 2.5–5 cm (1–2 in) of mulch between shrubs and perennials, tucking under overhanging shrubs for maximum coverage.

• *COMPOSTED BARK CHIPPINGS* are a good, green alternative when you want a very natural-looking mulch. These chippings have been ground up and left to partly decompose and don't hold as much water as peat. Cocoa shells are decorative and appear to repel slugs, snails and cats. It smells of chocolate but is, unfortunately, expensive and breaks down quickly, so needs reapplying each year.

• *CHUNKY BARK CHIPPINGS* are longer lasting, although quite expensive in England. We use these in our French garden as they are very cheap and readily available from the local supermarket. The local pine forests must do well out of the deal. The mulch smells lovely, but only the larger pieces are birdproof, so be prepared to sweep up paths after a good few beaks have rifled through it. The best grades last up to five years.

• *GRAVEL* is decorative and long lasting, but doesn't suit every planting style. Unless you put a membrane of plastic down and an edging first, it is likely to disappear into flowerbeds. Even then, earthworms will raise casts between the stones and seedlings of weeds will flourish. Cats don't seem to mind it either, unfortunately. As long as you're prepared to weed and rake, it's a long-lasting mulch.

SHEET MULCHES

For cutting down on regular chores, synthetic mulches are a good idea. They form a weedproof barrier and are usually made of perforated or woven material that lets rain and air through, but not weeds. They don't look good, so you need to cover them with chippings or gravel.

- Black polythene sheeting is the cheapest, but you must make holes once it is laid by stabbing with a garden fork. It tears easily and often shows through covering material if you walk on it.
- Perforated or slitted plastic costs more, but still rucks up and tears easily.

- Spun landscape fabric is stronger and durable. It needs anchoring down well.
- Woven fabric is the heaviest quality, more like matting, and the most expensive. It won't tear, and if you change your mind about where to mulch, you can take it up and move it. It will last for years as it doesn't rot.

PLANTING THROUGH MULCHING SHEETS

Place the sheet on the prepared soil and anchor it down. Stand the plants, still in pots, on the sheet and arrange them how you want them, before cutting the sheet. Cut a cross in the fabric where you want each plant to go. Peel back the corners, put in the plant and tuck the corners of the sheet back round the neck of the plant. Cover with chippings when planting is finished.

PLANT DISEASES

Fungal diseases affect the leaves of many plants and can be difficult to control. Where possible, grow varieties that have a disease resistance and remove affected leaves at the first sign of trouble. This will prevent the problem from spreading. Always collect up dead leaves, but don't use them for compost. If you need to use a spray, do so carefully, following the instructions on a still day, when rain is not due. See Appendix 1, page 151 for details of mildews, rust and leaf spot.

BENEFICIAL INSECTS

NAME OF INSECT	CHARACTERISTICS	WOULD LIKE TO EAT
LADYBIRD	Most are small red beetles with black spots. Larvae: long dark grey with yellow stripes.	Thousands of aphids (greenfly).
HOVERFLIES	Look like wasps, but don't buzz.	Thousands of aphids.
SPIDERS	Effective predators, even the smallest.	Thousands of aphids.
EARWIGS	Thin brown beetles with pincers.	Fruit tree pests and overwintering insect eggs.
BEETLES	Black shiny colour, 6 legs.	Soil pests including slugs, cabbage root fly.
LACEWING	Green or brown, like very delicate moths.	Thousands of aphids.

BIRD HELPERS

BIRD	LIKES TO EAT
ROBIN	Feed on soil pests, will follow you around when you are digging or raking, eating grubs.
THRUSH	Snails. Will crack them open on a favourite stone or path.
BLACKBIRD	Small caterpillars, insects.
BLUE TIT, GREAT TIT	Large quantities of greenfly.
GREEN WOODPECKER	Loves ants and larvae of wood-boring insects, beetles, moths and flies.
STARLING	Leatherjackets, wireworms, soil pests.
HOUSE MARTINS AND SWALLOWS (SUMMER VISITORS)	Insects on the wing.

ANIMAL HELPERS

NAME	EATS	ENCOURAGE THEM BY:
HEDGEHOG	Snails, slugs and other pests.	Avoiding moving piles of rubbish or compost in winter. Check bonfires before lighting. *Don't leave out bread and milk.*
FROGS	Slugs and insects.	Put in a pond or small water area with sloping sides for breeding.
NEWTS	Slugs and insects.	Spend most time out of water.
TOADS	Ants and slugs.	
SHREWS	Slugs and snails.	Leave compost undisturbed in winter.

COMMON DISEASES

DISEASE	PLANTS MOST AT RISK	FOUND	REMEDY
POWDERY MILDEW (FUNGAL DISEASE)	Roses, Michaelmas daisies.	Late summer and autumn, after a dry spell.	Mulch heavily in spring. Choose disease-resistant varieties. Control weeds which often harbour the spores.
RUST DISEASE	Roses, leeks, pelargoniums.	On foliage; looks like red or brown dots which spread to form larger patches.	Spray with fungicide. No real cure. Destroy affected foliage to prevent spread.
GREY MOULD	Tomatoes, plants in greenhouses and conservatories.	Mainly on dying leaves, but can affect any part of the plant.	Avoid overcrowding during dull, damp conditions and increase ventilation to greenhouses.
BROWN ROT	Fruit such as apples, on the tree or windfalls.	Rings of raised white spots growing in soft, brown, rotten patches of fruit.	Destroy affected fruit to limit the spread of spores. Pick off affected leaves.

COMMON PEST PROBLEMS AND SOLUTIONS

PEST	PLANTS MOST AT RISK	FOUND	REMEDY
Slugs and Snails	Plant foliage at night.	In damp shady places, under plants, under stones, down sides of paths.	Encourage birds, frogs (see above). Gather up by hand and drown in a bucket. Put down saucers of beer. Use (organic) slug pellets as a last resort, covered up to avoid being eaten by bircs. Cover individual plants with the tops of 2 litre plastic drink bottles with the lids off. Surround plants with ash, gravel or ground eggshells.
Greenfly	Roses, young, tender plants.	Tips of stems, flower buds, young leaves.	Encourage blue tits or biological predators. Wipe off tender stems. Spray selectively to avoid harming beneficial creatures.
Blackfly	Broad beans, elder.	Tips of young stems.	Remove by hand. Cut off affected stems.
Vine Weevils	Roots of plants and in pots of peaty mixtures. Primula, cyclamen and container plants. Rhododendron and evergreen leaves (adult weevils).	Larvae found around roots of plants, especially in pots and containers.	Biological control. Use a potting mixture that is pretreated with pesticide, if desperate.
Soil pests Leatherjackets, Cutworms, Wireworms	Newly planted vegetables and flowers.	Newly cultivated soil that was grassland. Common in vegetable plots.	Dig over newly cultivated ground in winter and turn over again to expose grub to the birds.
Winter Moths	Apple buds and shoots.	Fruit trees.	Fix grease bands round tree trunks in autumn. Flightless females will be caught when they crawl up to lay eggs.
Codling Moths Plum Fruit Moths	Apples, pears, plums.	Fruit trees.	Hang a pheromone trap. The piece of sticky card attracts the males, so that the females are not fertilised.

GETTING TO GRIPS WITH WEEDS

METHOD	EFFECTIVE AGAINST	BEST FOR	WHAT TO USE	WHEN	AIM	HINT
Hoeing	Annuals, perennials	Mass weeding or for plants in straight rows.	Dutch hoe (push-pull), draw hoe (chopping).	Warm dry weather.	Slice off weeds when small. Uproot seedlings.	Always rake up larger seedlings so that they don't re-root.
Hand weeding	Annuals, perennials	Congested borders.	Hand fork or border fork.	When soil is soft, moist.	Dig out annuals before seeding, remove perennial roots.	Don't put perennials on the compost, where they will regrow.
Watering can and weedkiller	Annuals, perennials	Clearing new ground where there are no plants to keep.	Contact or systemic weedkiller.	When weeds are growing vigorously.	Cover the foliage with a layer of fine drops.	Don't use the watering can for normal watering, or fertilising. Don't water so heavily that the water runs onto the soil.
Ready-to-use sprays	Annuals, perennials	Spot treating individual weeds or paving.	Systemic products based on glyphosate.	On vigorous weeds, not before rain.	Cover all the foliage with a layer of fine drops.	Wash off any accidental spraying on the wrong plant immediately.
Spot weeder	Perennials	Treating individual weeds when you can't use a spray.	Gel or aerosol or lawn stick (roll-on).	When weeds are growing vigorously.	Cover most of leaf area with gel or product.	Works best on dandelions, daisies and plantains.
Vinegar	Annuals, perennials	Treating individual weeds when you can't use a spray.	3 parts water to 1 part vinegar.	On young weeds in paths, paving, etc.	Cover all the foliage with a layer of fine drops.	Suppressant rather than permanent killer. Avoid using on lawns or in herbaceous beds.

SPRING JOBS

Trees, shrubs and climbers	Prune modern roses and clematis varieties that need it. Prune winter jasmine and spring-flowering shrubs as soon as flowers are finished. Weed, mulch and feed all woody plants. Plant hardy woody plants but delay planting marginally hardy ones until after last frost.	March to May
Pond	Divide water plants carefully, but not water lilies. Lift out plants and divide, replanting good portions. Don't empty the pond and don't disturb early newts, mating frogs or fish. Frogspawn should be undisturbed on the surface.	February/ March
Vegetables, salad and herbs	Fork over soil and rake in general purpose fertiliser. Cover soil with cloches for early sowings or with black plastic to warm up. Sow spring onions, lettuce, herbs. Plant out onion sets, shallots, garlic and hardy herb plants. Sow tomatoes indoors and prick out as soon as first true leaf opens. Put potatoes to chit in a dark place. Plant out.	February onwards March to early May
Lawns	Start mowing as soon as grass dries out enough with a high cut. Redefine edges for neatening with shears. Repair bare patches with turf or sowing grass seed. Rake out moss and aerate grass with lawn rake and fork. Fill any big holes with sand or compost. Delay feeding lawn until late spring.	February onwards
Hedges and fences	Clear weeds and ivy from bottom. Clip fast-growing hedges regularly from first growth, but try to avoid disturbing nesting birds.	February to April
Patios and containers	Clean patio slabs with water, weak detergent and a stiff broom. Wash containers to be used for potting on and clean containers that have been standing out all winter. Replace winter displays with spring bedding or pots of spring bulbs, temporarily arranged in larger containers.	February onwards
Flowerbeds and borders	Cut down dead stems and remove early weeds. Apply general purpose fertiliser and while soil is moist, add mulch. Leave foliage of bulbs for six weeks before tidying up. Plant new perennials out. When they show growth, push in twiggy sticks for support. Plant dahlia tubers well below the soil surface to avoid frost damage. Plant lily bulbs.	March onwards April

SUMMER MAINTENANCE

Trees, shrubs and climbers	Keep new climbers tied in until they start to grip supports on their own. Plant new trees, shrubs and climbers but make sure you don't break up the rootball. Water well for the rest of the summer. Deadhead roses regularly and check for disease. Remove affected leaves and dispose of them safely. Check for suckers growing on rootstock of roses, witch hazel and contorted hazel. Prune trained fan or cordon trees and cherries.	May to September September
Pond	Put tender floating water plants in pond. Regularly thin out excess waterweeds and skim off floating duckweed with a small net. Reduce blanket weed.	May onwards
Vegetables, salad and herbs	Continue sowing lettuce, radishes and spring onions. Sprinkle pelleted chicken manure between sowings. Dig up early potatoes. Sow baby carrots, beetroot, French and runner beans, peas. Put in supports as you plant. Plant tomatoes, courgettes, out after last frosts. Feed indoor tomatoes, peppers, cucumbers, etc. Remove sideshoots of upright tomatoes and keep tying in new growth. Clear up leaves and debris from crops as they mature.	May/ June onwards
Lawns	Avoid watering. Don't use fertilisers or treatments in dry weather. Raise blades of mower in hot weather and remove grass box. Don't give up mowing as upright weeds will invade the lawn. Move garden furniture around to save wear and tear.	June onwards
Hedges and fences	Continue clipping fast-growing hedges. Clip old, slow-growing, established hedges in late summer.	August/ September
Patios and containers	Replace spring bedding with tender plants for colourful displays. Check containers daily and water when they feel dry. Take hanging baskets down overnight and soak in a large bowl if they dry out. Remove dead heads regularly and move pots around to best effect.	June
Flowerbeds and borders	Keep up to date with weeding. Water newly planted perennials, put in annuals to fill gaps. Stake tall heavy plants and regularly cut off dead stems of perennials. Cut sweet peas regularly to encourage flowering. Sow wallflowers.	May onwards July/ August

Trees, shrubs and climbers	Plant woody trees and shrubs. Plant or move evergreens in early autumn. Cut back climbing plants which have finished flowering or secure firmly against wind damage.	September/ October
Pond	Cut back marginal plants to reduce the amount of rotting vegetation in winter. Regularly remove leaves with a net, or cover pond with netting until spring. Rake out some of the waterweed, if too rampant.	October
Vegetables, salad and herbs	Cover late crops with cloches or fleece for protection. Plant overwintering onions and green manure crops. Keep harvesting beans regularly. Pick any unripe tomatoes for ripening indoors. Put cloches over herbs to prolong the season.	September/ October
Lawns	Give lawns a low-nitrogen feed to encourage root growth. Rake out moss and when soil is moist, rake or spike lawn, as in spring. Brush coarse sand into holes for drainage channels. Remove leaves regularly and prepare ground for new lawns. Sow grass seed in early autumn and turf from now onwards.	September/ October
Hedges and fences	Continue clipping fast-growing hedges. Clip old, slow-growing, established hedges in late summer.	September
Patios and containers	Keep an eye on pots and move any plants you want to keep indoors or protect from bad weather. Replace annuals with winter pansies, ornamental cabbage, etc. Plant bulbs for next spring.	October
Flowerbeds and borders	Cut perennials back for a tidy garden, or leave stems for the winter to help beneficial insects and birds. Clear away leaves and weeds, clear summer bedding and plants, as above. Pile debris into compost bins, ready for mulch in spring. Plant out wallflowers and spring bulbs.	October

WINTER

Trees, shrubs and climbers	Remove old trees or stumps. Prune apple and pear trees while dormant. Don't snip around the edges; remove entire branches growing in the centre of the crown to let light in. Thin out and remove dead, diseased or damaged branches. Plant bare-rooted hedging and fruit canes.	November to February
Pond	Don't allow ice to stay in a solid sheet for more than 12 hours. Float a tennis ball to avoid total coverage. Don't smash ice as the fish or pond life will suffer.	November to February
Vegetables, salad and herbs	Dig over unplanted ground.	Nov. to February
Lawns	Keep raking the leaves and spiking.	
Hedges and fences	Get rid of ivy while it is easier to spot in a deciduous hedge.	
Patios and containers	Keep an eye on pots and protect from bad weather. Move to a sheltered spot if possible, or insulate pots and use horticultural fleece. Lag pots before they freeze! Don't wait and hope for the best. Plant winter pansies, ornamental cabbage, etc.	November
Flowerbeds and borders	Tidy up, removing leaves and weeds that linger, encouraging slugs and pests.	November to February

The lists below are a guide only; it's impossible to list every good plant. *Botanical names are given in italics*

EASILY GROWN ANNUALS
Ageratum
Alyssum
Californian poppy *Escholzia*
Candytuft *Iberis umbellate*
Clarkia
Convolvulus tricolor
Corn or field poppy *Papaver rhoeas*
Cornflower *Centaurea cyanus*
Cosmea *Cosmos*
Godetia
Love lies bleeding *Amaranthus caudatus*
Love-in-a-mist *Nigella damascene*
Mallow *Lavatera trimestris*
Nasturtium *Tropaeolum majus*
Opium poppy *Papaver somniferum*
Phlox drummondii

Pot marigold *Calendula officinalis*
Salvia
Sunflower *Helianthus annuus*
Tobacco flowers *Nicotiana*

GROUND COVER PLANTS
SHRUBS
Cotoneaster dammeri
Daphne retusa
Dogwood *Cornus*
Genista pilosa 'Vancouver Gold'
Hebe buxifolia
Hypericum calycinum
Juniper *Euonymus Fortunei* 'Silver Queen'
Potentilla
Rosa x jacksonii
Spindle tree *Euonymus*
Viburnum davidii

PERENNIALS
Arabis

Aubretia
Bergenia
Dianthus
Geranium macrorrhizum
Greater periwinkle *Vinka major*
Heather *Calluna vulgaris*
Lungwort *Pulmonaria*
Luzula sylvatica (grass)
Oxalis
Phlox
Polygonum affine
Saxifraga
Sedum
Stachys
Thymus
Veronica
SHRUBS FOR GOOD STRUCTURE AND COLOUR
Abelia
Abutilon
Acer
Aucuba
Berberis
Calluna

Ceanothus
Cordyline
Cornus
Cotinus
Cytisus
Deutzia
Euonymus
Garrya
Hebe
Ilex
Lavandula
Ligustrum
Mahonia
Malus
Pittosporum
Pyracantha
Rhus
Robinia
Rosa Rugosa
Viburnum

PLANTS WITH A GOOD SCENT
(*in addition to scented roses*)
Golden rayed lily
    Lilium auratum
Honeysuckle *Lonicera*
Lavender *Lavandula*

Mexican orange blossom
    Choisya
Mock orange
    Philadelphus
Night scented stock
Pink *Dianthus*
Rosemary
Scented leaf
    pelargonium
Summer Jasmine
    Jasminium
Sweet briar *Rosa*
    rubiginosa
Sweet pea *Lathyrus*
Sweet rocket *Hesperis*
    matronalis
Tobacco plant *Nicotiana*
Verbena
Wallflower *Erysimum*

WINTER SCENTED PLANTS
Daphne mezereum
Hyacinth
Mahonia
Sarococca humilis
Viburnum
Witch hazel

LOW ALLERGEN PLANTS
Delphinium
Hebe Autumn Glory
Double wild cherry
    Prunus avium
Viburnum tinus
Weigela florida
Bergenia
Campanula persicifolia
Judas tree *Cercis*

POISONOUS PLANTS
These are some plants
that you might need to
watch, as young
children will try
anything that looks
edible or attractive.
Not everything in the
garden is safe to eat!
Sweet pea
Laburnum
Iris
Foxglove
Amaryllis
Lupin
Clematis

GLOSSARY
OF GARDENING TERMS

• *ACID SOIL* has a pH content lower than 7.0. The majority of plants will grow on acid soil, while plants such as rhododendrons and heathers will not grow on anything other than acid soil.

• *AERATING* soil or ground, including lawns, means loosening it with tools or a machine to expose it more to the air and to moisture.

• *AERIAL ROOTS* are roots you find on plant stems above ground, for example on orchids and ivy.

• *ALKALINE SOIL* has a pH content higher than 7.0. With the exception of acid soil loving plants such as rhododendrons and ericas (heathers), the majority of plants thrive on slightly alkaline or neutral soils.

• *ALLERGENS* are substances that trigger allergic reactions. For example, pollen is an allergen as it can cause hay fever.

• *ALPINE* is a term used to describe any plant growing in the alpine zone, that is between the tree line (or the upper limits of tree growth) and the permanent snow line. Small plants growing on a rockery are also often called alpine plants.

• *ANNUAL* plants only live for one year, for example sweet peas and marigolds.

• *APHID* is the term used to describe a plant-louse, for example the greenfly, that infests and causes damage to plants.

• *ARCHITECTURAL PLANTS* such as mahonias, fatsias and yuccas, provide a strong, lasting, evergreen framework within a garden.

• *BEDDING PLANTS* are hardy, half-hardy or tender annuals, biennials or perennials, used to provide an attractive garden display.

• *BIENNIAL* plants need two years to complete their growing cycle, the first to form leaves, the second to flower, fructify (fruit and seed) and perish.

• *BIOLOGICAL CONTROL* is the introduction of natural predators in order to eradicate pests. For example, ladybirds are often used on plants to counteract aphids.

• *CANE* is a term used to describe the thin, often hollow, woody stems of plants. It is applied especially to bamboo and to the stems of raspberries, blackberries and loganberries.

• *CELLULOSE* is a carbohydrate that forms the main constituent of plant-cell walls and gives plants their shape and structure.

• *CHLOROPHYLL* is the green colouring matter in plants, essential to photosynthesis.

• *CLOCHE* was originally a bell-shaped glass cover, used to propagate plants or to protect tender plants or early crops from frosts. Nowadays cloches are made of glass or plastic sheeting of a wide range of sizes and lengths and are used to promote early growth in crops in open ground.

• *COMPOST* is formed organically from layers of garden refuse, including grass cuttings, and uncooked fruit and vegetable peelings, inside a compost bin or in a heap or an enclosure. Over the course of a season the materials rot down to form a rich, brown, crumbly humus to spread on garden plots to promote plant growth.

• *CONIFEROUS* meaning 'cone-bearing', is a term applied to shrubs and trees that are usually evergreen and have needle-like leaves. For example, spruces and pine trees are conifers.

• *CORM* is a bulblike, underground stem, often covered with paper-like skin. It is the plant's storage organ, and the bud at the top of the corm contains both shoots and new roots.

• *COTYLEDON* is the primary or seed-leaf that appears once germination has started. Sometimes, as in the case of broad beans, the seed-leaves remain underground, while the first shoot to appear above ground bears adult leaves, which are often quite different in shape. The onion seed-leaf looks like a blade of grass.

• *DECIDUOUS* trees and shrubs, unlike evergreens, shed their leaves at the end of the growing season, in order to minimise the loss of water to the plant and to protect it from low temperatures.

• *DIBBER* is the name given to any (wooden) peg or blunt-ended stick that can be used to make holes for (trans)planting bulbs, seeds or seedlings.

• *DORMANT* means lying inactive or resting and refers to the period when a plant stops developing, usually throughout autumn and winter.

• *EVERGREEN* trees and shrubs, unlike deciduous trees and shrubs, retain their leaves and foliage throughout the year.

• *FUNGICIDE* is a fungus-destroying substance, such as copper sulphate.

• *FUNGUS* generally speaking is a form of mould, a chlorophyll-free plant that feeds on organic matter. The term can also be used to describe plants such as the mushroom and the toadstool.

• *GERMINATION* is the first stage in the development of a plant from seed.

• *GRAFTING* is the process of inserting a shoot or bud from one plant into a slit in the stock of another, to produce an entirely new plant. Grafting is quite common with fruit trees and plants that are slow to produce roots by the usual method of propagation from cuttings.

• *HARDENING OFF* is the term used to describe the gradual acclimatisation of plants that have been grown in a heated greenhouse before spring. In late spring these tender and half-hardy plants are first placed in an unheated greenhouse or cold frame or even against a warm wall outside, then they are gradually exposed to normal air conditions, in order to avoid damage from frost or cold weather.

• *HARDY ANNUAL* plants flourish in the open even when there are frosts.

• *HERBACEOUS* plants do not have woody stems. Herbaceous borders usually consist of perennial flowering plants that die down each autumn but reappear in the following spring.

• *HUMUS* is the rich, dark brown material that results from decomposed plants, such as you find in leaf mould or well-rotted compost.

• *HYBRID* is the term used for a plant formed by crossing two different species or varieties.

• *INSECTICIDE* is a substance used to kill insects that are harmful to plants.

• *LAYERING* is the process of fastening into the soil a shoot from a plant already growing, so that the shoot also strikes root itself.

• *LEACHING* is the process of removing soluble matter from soil by allowing water to percolate through it.

• *LEAF MOULD* is soil that consists mainly of decomposed leaves. Also known as leaf soil, it is an extremely rich compost that promotes successful, healthy growth in plants. Although any deciduous leaves can be used to make leaf mould, oak and beech leaves are the most suitable.

• *LEGUMINOUS* plants, such as peas and beans, have seeds in pods.

- *LIGNIN* is the material in the cell walls of woody plants that make them stiff.
- *LIME* is an important source of calcium and is sometimes used as a fertiliser, to neutralise soil that is too acid.
- *LOAM* is a mineral-rich, fertile soil consisting of a blend of clay, sand and decayed vegetable matter.
- *MILDEW* is a destructive growth of tiny fungi on plants and surfaces exposed to damp conditions.
- *MULCH* can consist of compost, leaf mould, straw, sawdust or peat. It is spread around the base of plants to retain moisture, protect roots and keep down weeds.
- *NECTAR* is a sweet fluid produced by plants to attract insects, in order to promote pollination. Bees make nectar into honey.
- *NEUTRAL SOIL* has a pH of between 6.5 and 7.0 and is neither acid nor alkaline.
- *NODE* is the term used to describe a knob on a root or a branch, where shoots, buds and leaves appear.
- *PERENNIAL* plants, usually herbaceous/non-woody, live for several years.
- *PESTICIDE* like insecticide is a substance for destroying pests, mainly insects.
- *PH* readings give you the acidity or alkalinity of the water in the soil, using the pH scale. A reading of 7.0 means the soil is neutral; below 7.0 means more acid soil, above it means more alkaline.
- *PHOTOSYNTHESIS* is the process plants use to convert sunlight and water into energy. The green pigment — or chlorophyll — traps the sunlight, then turns the carbon dioxide from the air and the water from the soil into carbohydrates. These are stored as starchy substances in the leaves and roots and are then gradually released to give the plant a continuing source of energy.
- *POLLINATION* occurs when plants are fertilised or sprinkled with pollen, artificially by hand or naturally by the wind, insects or gravity.
- *PRICKING OUT* is the term used for planting out seedlings in rows of small holes pricked in the soil using, for example, your finger, a pencil or a knitting needle.
- *PROPAGATION* is the reproduction of plants from seed or, more commonly, using cuttings from the parent plant.
- *PRUNING* plants, especially those with woody stems, is used to remove dead wood and/or to promote new growth. It is also used to train or shape plants.
- *RHIZOMES* are stems that remain below ground but continue to grow horizontally and form a food reserve for the plant. In iris rhizomes the terminal bud turns up and produces flowers and leaves above ground.
- *ROTATION OF CROPS* is the growing of different crops in a regular order on the same plot of land, in order to avoid exhausting the soil's reserves of minerals.
- *SPORE* is the tiny, single reproductive cell of plants like mosses, fungi and ferns.
- *STERILE* plants generally never seed. For example, in many double-flowered plants the reproductive organs have become petals, so the plant cannot seed.
- *SUCCULENT* plants, such as cacti, have thick, fleshy stems or leaves and flourish in very dry conditions.
- *SUCKER* is used to describe any shoot on a plant that comes from below ground level and usually from the root of the plant.
- *TAPROOT* is the central descending root of a plant.
- *TENDER* plants are not resistant to frost.
- *TILTH* is crumbly, fine, cultivated soil at surface level.
- *TOP DRESSING* means adding fresh soil or compost around the base of plants.
- *TRANSPIRATION* is continual loss of water through leaves and stem surfaces.
- *TRANSPLANTING* means relocating plants in the garden to give them more space or a better aspect for growth.
- *TRENCHES* are long, narrow furrows, usually quite deep, for the cultivation of certain types of vegetables, such as potatoes and runner beans, and flowers, for example sweat peas.
- *TRUSS* is the term used to describe a cluster of fruit, such as tomatoes, or flowers.
- *TUBERS* are the short, thick rounded parts of the stem or rhizome (see above), in plants such as potatoes and dahlias.
- *VARIEGATED* leaves or petals are so-called because they have spotted or striped patterns in contrasting colours.